D0016270

The Lady Mechanic's
Total Car Care
for the Clueless

Ren Volpe

St. Martin's Griffin
New York

Design by Diane Hobbing of Snap-Haus Graphics

All drawings Copyright © 1998 by Kris Kovick

Library of Congress Cataloging-in-Publication Data

Volpe, Ren.
  The lady mechanic's total car care for the clueless / by Ren Volpe.—1st ed.
    p. cm
    Includes index.
    ISBN 0-312-18733-5
    1. Automobiles—Maintenance and repair—Amateurs' manuals.   2. Women automobile drivers.   I. Title.
TL 152.V65   1998
629.28'722—dc21   98-9435
                                                              CIP

First St. Martin's Griffin Edition: July 1998
10   9   8   7   6   5   4   3   2   1

For Kris Kovick
(who wisely married a mechanic)
&
Gina, Nonda, and Jane Volpe
(three strong, wonderful women)

Acknowledgments

I want to acknowledge the hundreds of women who have taken my auto-repair class over the years. It was at the prompting of my students that I had the idea to write a car book in the first place. A thousand thanks to my mother, Jane Volpe, and my sisters Nonda and Gina, for never saying, "You can't do that" (whatever crazy *that* I was attempting at the time). Big kisses for Kris Kovick and Dan O'Connell for constantly telling me that I could write. Terri Hogan, ace mechanic, was a great help in proofreading, and thanks also to the many folks along the way who taught me a lot of what I know, especially George Gyi and Robin Schneider at SF Auto Repair Center in San Francisco. And also special thanks to Nora Frala, just for being Nora.

Contents

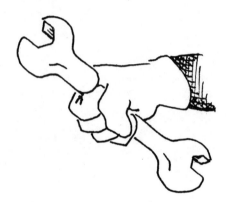

Introduction

Like it or not, most of us are dependent on automobiles. These complicated machines need regular maintenance, and even when they get it, sometimes they just stop working, usually when you're on your way to someplace important. What a drag. Even if your car starts driving funny or breaks down, you still need to get there. It can be scary and frustrating. Fortunately, learning about cars is easier than you might think.

The more you know about your own car, the greater your peace of mind. You don't need to be a mechanical genius to understand the basics of owning and maintaining a car. I'm not talking about buying tools and learning how to fix your car. Just a little knowledge can save you a great deal of hassle and money.

Mechanics have a bad rap; and sometimes it's deserved. It's a thin line between thievery and incompetence. While it may be true that there are unscrupulous mechanics, it is certainly true that if you don't know anything about your car, there's no way to know whether you've been ripped off. Knowledge is power. The more you know, the less chance there is of your being cheated when it comes to repairs. But even if you're not getting ripped off, auto repair is expensive. And if you're a woman, there's a good chance you've experienced male mechanics talking to you like you're an idiot. Who needs it?

I didn't, and nine years ago I decided to do something about it. Maybe I had a macho complex, but I really did want to learn how to fix cars. I had visions of driving across the country without a care in the world. If my car broke down in the middle of the desert, no problem; I'd be able to handle it. Before I became a mechanic, I drove old cars that broke down all the time. I was completely stressed out every time I heard a new squeak or rattle. I hated bringing my car to garages, because I suspected I was being cheated but I didn't know enough to prove it.

I was the last person anyone expected to become an auto mechanic. I grew up in Manhattan, where having a car is a full-time job, so I didn't bother learning how to drive until I was twenty. I attended trade school in upstate New York after graduating from college with a degree in philosophy. Picture this: a blonde, intellectual city girl who knew nothing about engines. Well, almost nothing. As a child I compulsively took things apart: Barbie dolls, clocks, old bicycles, you name it, but I often couldn't get them back together again. When I told my parents I was learning to be an auto mechanic, my father said, without missing a beat, "But you have no mechanical aptitude!" Thanks for the encouragement, Dad. The boys in my trade school had been taking things apart and putting them back together since they could walk. Things like their dad's tractor. They probably had plenty of help and encouragement, too.

Trade school was a constant battle. The boys resented my presence and the teachers couldn't figure out why I was there. One kid spat at my feet every time he walked by. Another kicked my tools across the shop whenever he got the chance. I had a relentless peanut gallery of boys around any car I was working on. They'd tell me what I was doing wrong or offer unsolicited advice. After a few frustrating months of seemingly innocuous attempts to "help" me (I'm *learning*, remember?), I finally blew up and shouted, "Men have been taking tools out of women's hands for thousands of years, I'll do it myself, goddamnit!" Then they really thought I was crazy. But I persevered, and by the end of the course I was even friends with some of those boys.

Trade school taught me the basics, but most of what I know I learned on the job. In this field there are always new things to learn. Being a mechanic, I've had my share of trials and tribulations, which any woman in a male-dominated field would recognize. Learning to be a good mechanic takes at least as long as studying to be a doctor. Automotive technology changes every year, and the number of makes and models in the past ten years alone is dizzying. Many mechanics, like doctors, specialize. Some fix only Japanese cars, or work only on transmissions, for example. The days of the backyard mechanic are quickly fading. So it's not surprising to hear people say, "New cars are so complicated, I don't even want to open the hood." This is absurd. The cost of auto repair is so high you can't afford *not* to pay attention to your car's health.

You don't have to be a mechanic, or even know how an engine works, to take good care of your car. A little curiosity and willingness can go a long way. The important thing to remember is that the reason you don't know about cars is not because you're a woman. It's because you've never been taught. Knowing where to add oil is not innate knowledge. Men aren't born knowing this stuff, either. They also had to be shown, at one point or another. Understanding what's going on with your car is your own choice, and you can learn as much or as little as you want. More than half of the cars that get towed into shops are there for repairs that could have been prevented by regular maintenance—reason enough to learn a little.

I created this book out of necessity. After more than five years of teaching basic auto maintenance and mechanics classes for women, I was still not able to find a book to use in the class. Most car books either presuppose heaps of previous knowledge or are 400 pages long and too technical for the average car owner. In this book I try not to use terms without explaining what they mean. (Consult the glossary at the back of the book if there's a word you don't know.)

This book will teach you how to care for your car, not how to repair it. Keep it in your glove compartment or trunk. If you find yourself on the side of the road with a flat tire and feel a little shaky about how to change it, you can look at the illustrations and brush up before you begin. You may want to read the entire manual all at once to get a good overview, or read each part as it becomes relevant to you and your car. If you are worried about safety (yours or your car's), read Chapter I on safety to get a better idea of what's dangerous and what's not.

Oh yeah, about the title. It's sort of tongue in cheek, because the truth is, I'm really not very ladylike. But one afternoon I was walking around the corner to the machine shop carrying a couple of brake rotors when a guy leaned out his car window and shouted, "Hey look, a lady mechanic!" as if he had just spotted some rare bird. It was the end of a very long, hot day, and I was filthy and tired. I certainly didn't look like a lady, so I found this to be extremely amusing. I still think it's funny, but not in a cute way, if you know what I mean.

Happy Trails!

Chapter I

Safety

What's Dangerous and What's Not, In and Around Your Car

Because cars are so complex you might have concerns about safety. You may be afraid of endangering yourself by attempting a repair, or about damaging your car. In this book you will not learn how to fix cars, so don't worry. Everything I'm teaching you is about keeping you and your car safe. The best advice I can give you about car safety is to drive defensively and beware of jerks on the road. More people get injured from car accidents than anything else. In fact, I can't think of a single person who has hurt herself checking her car's fluids.

Here is a list of basic things you should know about your car regarding safety. Some of them are obvious and simply employ common sense, and some may be new to you.

Safety Around Fans and Belts

When looking under the hood of your car, remove or tie back any dangling clothing, hair, or jewelry, as these could get caught in the fan or the belts. Some cars have electric fans that can go on even when the car is not running and the key is out of the ignition.

Hot and Wet Things: Cooling-System Safety

Never take the radiator cap off when the engine is hot. The radiator is pressurized, and the coolant could spray out and scald you. When the car is hot, you *can* add coolant to the plastic reservoir/overflow tank. If you must add coolant to the radiator when the engine is warm, use a few rags between your hand and the cap and open slowly, as if you were opening a bottle of soda someone had just shaken up. If you have a German car (VW, Audi, etc.) or a Volvo, the plastic tank is also under pressure, so take special care when adding coolant. Watch out for coolant leaks in your garage or driveway. Coolant is toxic, but cats and dogs seem to like the sweet taste of ethylene glycol.

Heat and Fumes: Exhaust-System Safety

The exhaust on your car is very hot and can burn you. The exhaust pipe under the car runs the length of the car, and under the hood the exhaust manifold is very hot. The exhaust manifold is where exhaust comes out of your engine into the exhaust pipe. The exhaust system is usually a rusty reddish-brown color, darker than other metal parts of your engine. If you are unsure whether something is too hot to touch, feel the air a few inches away before putting your fingers on it. Do not run your car in a garage or enclosed area that doesn't have good ventilation. Carbon monoxide is odorless and poisonous and it can kill you if you breathe enough of it.

Electricity: Battery Safety

Batteries are dangerous if they "arc," or make sparks, because the sparks can cause a fire. The electricity from your battery is not enough to hurt you, although if you do arc the battery you'll probably jump back and bang your head on the hood, which will hurt a lot. Electricity needs a circuit, or circle, to flow. You will arc the battery if you complete the electrical circuit by touching the positive post to the negative post. The battery posts are the two small, round, metal parts that protrude from the top of the battery. This is why the positive battery post often has a little plastic cover on it. You can also arc the battery by touching the positive post to any other metal part of the engine or frame. Read Chapter 6 on jump-starting for more information about how to hook up jumper cables correctly.

Under the Car: Jack Safety

The jack that comes with your car is only for changing tires. Never get underneath a car that is supported only by a tire-changing jack! Mechanics have a different type of jack and special jack stands used for working underneath cars. You can read about how to jack up your car safely in Chapter 5, which will also show you, step by step, how to change a flat tire.

Cars Blowing Up

"I'm afraid my engine will blow up" seems to be a particularly vivid fear among drivers, but it is very rare for cars to blow up. Maybe we've all seen too many action movies. Cars *can* blow up after rolling over a cliff, but if you've driven off a steep cliff you're already in trouble. Cars *can* catch on fire (usually due to electrical problems), but even then it's highly unlikely that your car will blow up. The expression "blowing a head gasket" means that the gasket (seal) between the top half and the bottom half of the engine fails, allowing air and/or coolant to leak into the cylinders. A blown head gasket will cause a car to run rough and lose power, and you may see billowing clouds of white smoke at the tailpipe. It sounds dramatic, but nothing actually blows up.

Fire

To be on the safe side, never keep gasoline in a container in your car—even in the trunk—because gasoline fumes can ignite very easily. Electrical fires do occur in cars, although it's not extremely common. The old air-cooled Volkswagen Bugs and buses did catch on fire with some frequency, and Ford had problems with side mounted gas tanks on some pickup trucks. (They were all recalled.) But don't lose sleep over the possibility of your car catching on fire. If you do suspect there is a fire in the engine compartment, do not open the hood! This will only give the fire oxygen and make it burn faster. Turn off the ignition right away, unlatch the hood from inside the car (so when the fire department comes they can open the hood), but keep the hood closed. Move away from the car and call the fire department.

Road Rage

Aggressive driving is sort of a hobby with Americans, and studies show that this newly named phenomenon causes more than half of all automobile accidents. For those concerned with safety, your best bet is to stay clear of aggressive drivers (speeders, tailgaters, and drivers who engage in honking and shouting matches on the road). Be especially careful whom you flip off or cut off on the road, because even if they don't have a gun, a car can be used as a weapon.

Chapter 2

Dashboard Lights and Gauges

What They Mean and What to Do If They Come On

Seeing Red (or Yellow): Checking the Dashboard Lights and Gauges

There is no dashboard light that means "ignore me." Red signifies "danger" or "stop" in our culture. Your dashboard lights are red because they are meant to catch your attention immediately. The driver who ignores this in-your-face message is cruising for problems. Yellow lights on the dashboard are reminder, or "get it checked soon," lights. They tell you that something needs to be checked out or serviced soon, but not necessarily right away.

You've probably noticed that when you first get in your car and turn the key, all the dashboard lights blink on for a few seconds. This is supposed to happen. It is a way to test that all the warning lights are working. If you turn the key and the oil light doesn't go on, for instance, you need to get it fixed right away (ask your mechanic to check the oil-sending unit first). What happens if you hit a huge pothole and get a hole in the oil pan? All the oil would leak out and you wouldn't know it until it was too late. In this case, too late means a new engine and a few thousand dollars.

The dials on the analog gauges (circular with a pointer) on the dashboard will not give a reading until the engine is running, so you can check the gauges only with the engine on.

Make it a habit to glance at the dashlights and gauges when you first start the car and periodically while on the road. In this chapter you will learn what each of your car's dash lights means and what to check if any of them comes on.

Gas Gauge

This is an easy one. If you don't know what a gas gauge is or what it does, turn in your license, you have no business behind the wheel.

There are at least two good reasons to pay attention to your gas gauge beyond the obvious fear of running out of gas (although I can think of more than a couple of customers who have had their cars towed in, and the problem was they were out of gas). First, make it a habit not to drive your car when it's close to empty on the gas gauge. If there is any sediment or rust at the bottom of the gas tank, it will get sucked into the fuel system and can cause expensive problems.

Another reason to pay attention to the gas gauge is because it tells you how much gas your engine is using. It's a good idea to calculate the fuel mileage once in a while. Some problems may affect gas mileage, but the car will drive just fine. If you never calculate the gas mileage, you may be spending more on gas than you need to.

Poor gas mileage is an indication of a problem. Don't assume you "just need a tune-up." You may be spending money for something that won't fix the problem. Explain why you are bringing the car in.

How to figure out your gas mileage:

1. Fill the tank and jot down the exact odometer mileage.
2. Record the mileage when the tank is three-quarters empty.
3. Fill the tank again and write down exactly how many gallons it took.
4. Subtract the first mileage from the second mileage. Divide this by the number of gallons of gasoline you bought the second time. Don't forget that city driving and highway driving will give different results. Stop-and-go driving and short trips use more gas.

Oil Light or Gauge

Without oil and oil pressure to lubricate your engine, it would seize up; that is, all the metal parts would melt together. Last time I checked, new engines weren't cheap, either. The good news is, all cars have either a warning light or a gauge that tells you if the oil is circulating inside the engine. There's no excuse for ruining a perfectly good engine by driving it without oil. If the oil light comes on, or the oil gauge drops to zero, STOP DRIVING! **Don't even** drive to the next exit, unless of course you have extra money lying around you'd like to spend on a new engine. Without oil pressure you can ruin an engine in a few minutes. This is pretty serious stuff.

If the oil light comes on, *stop driving*, pull over to the side of the road, and turn off the engine. Check your oil with the car parked on level ground and the engine off. Do not add oil without checking the dipstick first (see page 39). Pull the dipstick out, then wipe it clean with a rag, and put it back in, being sure it is in all the way. Pull it out again and see if you need to add any oil. If the oil is low, add only a little at a time. You can always add more oil, but if you put in too much you can't get it out easily. Don't forget to put the filler cap on and put the dipstick back in. If the light goes off when you start the car, you can drive safely. On most cars the light won't come on until you are two quarts or more low, so there is a good chance you have an oil leak somewhere. Make an appointment with your mechanic to find out why the engine was so low on oil.

If the oil light comes on and there *is* enough oil in the engine, it's time to call a tow truck. There may be enough oil in the engine, but the pump that makes it circulate (the oil pump) is not working. It's always possible that the light or gauge may be broken, but driving with the oil light on can be expensive risk-taking.

Temperature Gauge (Overheating)

All cars have a gauge that measures the temperature of the coolant in the engine block. The cooling system uses a 50/50 mixture of antifreeze and water to keep the engine cool. Temperatures inside an engine can reach a few thousand degrees. If the cooling system isn't working properly and your car overheats, you can either "blow the head gasket" (damage the seal between the top and bottom half of the engine) or crack the cylinder head. Both are very expensive to repair.

Do not drive your car with the temperature gauge in the red zone. It takes only a few minutes to cause serious and expensive damage once your engine is too hot. Remember: Red means stop.

If the temperature gauge starts approaching the red mark, first turn off the air conditioner (if it's on) and turn the heat on high. Then pull over and turn off the engine. If you see steam coming from under the hood, wait about five minutes for the engine to cool down a little, then check the coolant. Never open the radiator cap when the car is hot! You can add coolant to the plastic reservoir when the car is hot, though. Add water and antifreeze (in a pinch one or the other is OK) to the coolant reservoir. You will find this reservoir (also called an overflow tank) by following the small hose that goes from the top of the radiator near the radiator cap to the plastic bottle. On German cars and Volvos the plastic coolant reservoir tank is also pressurized. You have to wait for the engine to cool down before adding water.

Low coolant level is one of the things that can cause overheating. The only reason the coolant would be very low is a coolant leak (or if it hasn't been checked in a million years). Fill the overflow tank and take your car in to your mechanic and get the cooling system "pressure checked" to find the source of the leak. Remember that leaks never fix themselves; in fact they usually get worse over time.

If your car is overheating and the coolant is full, the problem lies elsewhere in the cooling system. There may be a broken or loose water pump belt, a thermostat that's stuck closed, or an electric cooling fan that isn't coming on. Wait for the engine to cool down and drive to a

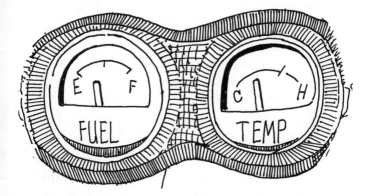

garage, stopping and waiting as often as you need to to keep the temperature gauge from going into the red zone.

Brake Light

When it comes to brakes, don't mess around. Ignoring the brake light will not only cost you, but it's not safe to drive when the brake light is on.

There are only two things that can cause the brake light to come on: either the parking brake is engaged or the brake fluid is low. If you notice the brake light on, first make sure you're not driving with the parking brake on. If that's not the cause, then check the brake fluid. You don't have to pull over immediately, as you do when the oil light comes on or the car is overheating, but don't wait until next week, either! Check it right away the next time you stop the car.

The brake fluid reservoir (called the brake master cylinder) is located at the rear of the engine compartment, to your right as you face the front of the car. Imagine where your foot would be if it went all the way through to the engine. Add brake fluid to the Full line. The light should go out, but you're not done yet! Make an appointment to get the brakes checked and find out why the fluid level was so low. There may be a leak, the rear brakes may need an adjustment (drum brakes only), or the pads may be very worn.

The brake light does not come on to remind you to get the brakes checked. The brakes may be completely worn and making an awful grinding metal noise, but the brake light will not come on unless the brake fluid also happens to be low. Get the brakes checked once a year, no matter what.

ABS (Antilock Brake System) Light

Low brake-fluid level will cause the ABS light to stay on. First check the brake fluid and fill as needed. The antilock brake sensors can also become caked with dirt, or one of the brake calipers may be sticking, causing the light to go on. Make an appointment to get the brakes checked!

Charge/Battery Light or Gauge

The charging system (alternator and voltage regulator) supplies the electricity for your car and recharges the battery when the engine is running. Your car uses electricity for all the accessories (lights, radio, etc.) More important, the engine needs electricity for the spark that ignites the gasoline that powers the car. The alternator is driven by a belt that turns when the engine is running.

All dashboards have a charge light or a gauge. It says Charge (or Chg) or Battery, or there is a picture of a battery. It is somewhat misnamed, because a dead battery will not trip the light. The battery light only goes on when the charging system isn't working.

The light will go on if the alternator belt is loose or broken or if the alternator itself is busted. *It does not mean you have a dead battery* (yet). It means there is a problem with the charging system. If you ignore this warning light, you *will* have a dead battery, as well as the original charging-system problem. Even worse, your car will actually stop running. Kaput. Just like that. The engine will quit and will not even crank when you turn the key. The lights won't work. A jump-start will not get you out of this bind. The minute you remove the jumper cables the engine will stop running again—there is no electricity in the battery and the alternator is not charging. In a pinch you can get the battery recharged so you have enough electricity to get home or to your favorite mechanic.

If the battery light stays on, or the gauge reads "discharge," you need to see your mechanic: The charging system is not working. You are driving on the battery electricity alone, which will last only a limited amount of time, maybe a couple of hours, depending on how much electricity is left in the battery. You can still drive, but you must conserve electricity by using only the accessories you absolutely need. Turn off the radio, the defroster, and the lights. Try not to turn the engine off and restart it more than is necessary, because starting your engine uses up a great deal of battery electricity.

On cars with a gauge on the dashboard instead of a light, you will see a D on one side and a C on the other, which means "discharge" and "charge," respectively. The needle will fluctuate slightly, but it should stay in the middle or point to the "charge" side of the dial. It will give a reading only when the engine is on. A gauge that reads "discharge" indicates a problem in the charging system.

On some cars the brake light will also go on when the charging-system light goes on. This doesn't mean there is a problem with both the charging and the brake systems. The lights are just wired to go on at the same time.

Check-Engine and/or Service-Engine-Soon Light

All modern cars have a "check-engine" light. It either says "check engine," or there is a little picture of an engine on it. The check-engine light is the voice of the car's computer. It tells the driver that the computer has sensed a problem somewhere in the fuel, ignition, or emissions systems. You may not notice anything different about the way your car performs (except for poor fuel mileage), but the computer can sense small problems before they become big ones. If the check-engine light comes on, it's time to see your mechanic.

A mechanic will not be able to tell you why the light is on without doing a little diagnostic work. When the car's computer (also called the ECM—electronic control module—or ECU—electronic control unit) senses a problem, it stores, or remembers, a "trouble" or "fault" code. Mechanics use a device called a scanner to retrieve these codes and find out what's wrong with the car.

Occasionally a check-engine light will flash on and then go off by itself. Don't stress too much about this. But when the light stays on, or consistently flashes on and off, make an appointment to have it checked out.

"Service engine soon" means the same thing on some cars as the check-engine light. Or it may simply mean it's time for an oil change or major service. Consult the owner's manual for your particular car.

Emissions Lights: 02, Oxygen Sensor, or EGR Service

Your car may also have a light that reads Emissions, 02 or Oxygen Sensor or EGR (exhaust gas recirculation) Service. These are typically maintenance reminder lights. It's not a big deal and doesn't mean your car is about to break down. Emissions lights are usually mileage sensitive (they are programmed to go on at a certain mileage, commonly at 60,000 miles). Make an appointment to have the emission system checked and the light turned off. Sometimes turning this dashboard light off is as simple as pressing a cleverly hidden button, but some cars are designed in such a way that turning the light off is a real headache. Emissions components on cars are warrantied for either five years or 50,000 miles (whichever comes first), or seven years or 70,000 miles (whichever comes first), depending on the part. Call the dealer before paying for repairs that may be covered under warranty.

Air Bag Light

Cars equipped with air bags have a dashboard light that will stay lit if there is a problem with the air bag system. A short circuit or a computer problem can cause this light to go on and stay on, indicating that the air bag may not work properly in the event of a crash. If your car is less than five years old, has gone fewer than 50,000 miles, or is still under warranty, the dealer should fix it for free.

Bulb Light

Finally, some cars have a bulb light, or a picture of a bulb with an x through it, indicating that a turn signal, brake light, or taillight bulb has burned out.

Chapter 3

Fuses

What Is a Fuse?

A fuse is a tiny wire that electricity passes through. Fuses are used to protect electrical equipment on your car, the way a surge protector protects your computer at home. Almost everything that uses electricity in your car is fused—radio, clock, fuel pump, headlights, etc. The electrical devices on your car can only handle a certain amount of electricity. The wire in the fuse will break (or "blow") if too much electricity flows through it, so the electricity cannot reach the device and damage it.

What Happens If a Fuse Blows?

Fuses are inexpensive and easy to replace, so it's not a big deal when a fuse blows. You can easily replace a blown fuse yourself. They cost about twenty-five cents each, or a few dollars for a package of assorted fuses.

When a fuse blows, electricity can no longer reach the device the fuse protects. What you will notice is something no longer works. If any of the accessories stop working, you should first check the fuse. Often one fuse protects more than one device: if the horn, the dome light, and the cigarette lighter all stop working at the same time, there's a good chance a fuse is the culprit.

How to Replace a Fuse

There's no reason to take the morning off work, make an appointment with your mechanic, and stress about how much it's going to cost if the problem is only a blown fuse. I wouldn't explain how to change a fuse if it was difficult. It's really easy, I promise.

First, you have to find the fuse box. It is usually under the dashboard to the left of the steering wheel. There may be a plastic cover you have to pull down or open in order to access the fuses. Some fuse boxes are located in the engine compartment. Check your owner's manual for the exact location. Some cars have more than one fuse box, one inside the car and one in the engine compartment.

The fuse box will have a label with a list of what each fuse is for and what size (amperage) each fuse should be. Fuses have different amperage ratings. An amp is a measurement of electrical pressure. A 15-amp fuse will blow if more than 15 amps passes through it. You should always replace a fuse with the same size fuse. If you replace a fuse with a smaller one it will blow right away. If you replace a fuse with a bigger amperage fuse you run the risk of damaging something much more expensive than the fuse—the device it's meant to protect. Never replace a fuse with a different size fuse!

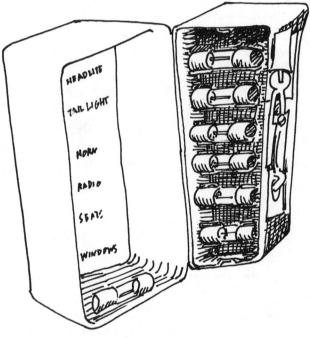

A FUSE BOX.

You might have to pull the fuse out in order to see if it is broken. If you can't pull it out with your fingers, there is a small plastic fuse puller in the fuse box for this purpose. Look at the thin strip of metal wire inside the fuse. If it is broken (looks like a broken filament inside a light bulb), replace the fuse.

It's a good idea to carry a few extra fuses in your car. There should also be some spare fuses in the fuse box. Different cars use different types of fuses. Pull one out of your fuse box and bring it with you into the parts shop to match it up.

Chapter 4

Checking Fluids—Yes, by Yourself

Why You Should Check Your Own Fluids

You should check your car's fluids at least every other time you fill your tank up with gas, and definitely before you go on a drive of any length. Once you become adept at this series of checks, it will take less than five minutes. I promise.

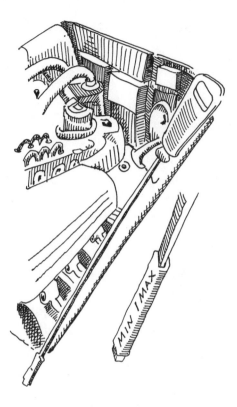

DIPSTICK FOR CHECKING OIL.

People are amazed to learn that it's not normal for a car's fluids to be low. If everything is properly sealed, the fluids (except gas), don't get used up. It's a closed system; they shouldn't go anywhere. Low fluid level is a sign that something is wrong (a leak is usually the culprit). The exceptions are brake fluid and windshield-washer fluid. Over time, as the brakes wear, the brake-fluid level will lower *slowly*. This is normal. If you have to add brake fluid every few weeks it means there is a leak. Get the brakes checked right away! The windshield-washer fluid also needs to be replenished as you use it.

Check your fluids regularly. It is a good way to keep tabs on how your car's systems are working. You can catch problems before they become severe enough to leave you stranded. For instance, say you check the coolant every week and notice it hardly ever needs topping off (adding a little). One week you check it, though, you notice that the coolant reservoir is very low. You fill it and decide to check it again the next morning. The next day it is low again. You correctly guess that you have a coolant leak and bring the car to the shop. Had you never checked, you would have gotten stuck in traffic when your car overheated and caused serious and expensive damage to your engine. The first time you check all your fluids some of them may be low, perhaps because they haven't been checked in a long while.

When putting fluids in your engine, always use a funnel if there is any possibility of spilling. Spilled oil on the engine can cause a nasty smell as it burns off, and it will look like as if you have a leak. You can use the same funnel for different fluids, just clean the funnel with a rag between uses.

If you still have questions about where things are under the hood after reading this chapter and looking through the owner's manual, don't be embarrassed to ask your mechanic to show you where everything is. If you are not sure, don't guess and don't assume the helpful-man-on-the-street knows more than you. He may be bluffing to impress you. One customer damaged her engine by allowing some "helpful onlookers" to add coolant to her over-heating engine. The problem was, they poured a gallon of antifreeze into the oil filler hole! She wasn't happy.

Manufacturers are trying to make cars more user-friendly. Many cars have labels on all the dipsticks and filler caps. If yours doesn't, take notes or draw a picture to help you remember where everything is.

Fluids

There are eleven possible fluids your car may have, depending on what type and model you own.

Automatic-transmission fluid (ATF): Lubricates the gears inside the automatic transmission. Used only in cars with an automatic transmission.

Battery fluid (electrolyte): Holds the electrical charge in the battery. Used in all cars.

Brake fluid: Helps the driver stop the car. Used in all cars.

Clutch fluid: Connects the clutch pedal to the transmission. This system is different from the brake system, although it also uses brake fluid. Used in some cars with a manual transmission. Cars with a clutch cable do not use this fluid.

Differential fluid (gear oil): Lubricates the gears inside the differential. Used only in rear-wheel-drive cars.

Gasoline: The fuel that burns inside the engine to create the power that makes your car go. Used in all cars except electric cars.

Manual-transmission fluid: Lubricates the gears inside the manual transmission. Used in all stick-shift cars. Some cars use motor oil, some use 90-weight, and some use ATF in the manual transmission.

Oil: Lubricates the moving metal parts inside the engine. It also helps to cool the engine. All cars use motor oil except electric cars.

Power-steering fluid: Makes steering easier. Used only in cars with power steering.

Radiator fluid (coolant): Keeps the engine cool. Used in all cars except old air-cooled VW Bugs and Buses.

Windshield-washer fluid: Cleans the windshield. Used in all cars.

Gasoline

What Does the Gas Do?

As you already know, gasoline is the fuel that makes the engine run. After you pump it in at the gas station, it is stored in the gas tank at the back of the car. The fuel pump pumps it to the engine. Along the way it gets filtered by the fuel filter, which filters out dirt and particles. Cars either have a carburetor *or* a fuel-injection system, which mixes the fuel with air and delivers it to the engine's cylinders. Inside the cylinder an electric spark ignites the air/fuel mixture and *kaboom!*—the heat energy from the burning gasoline makes your car go.

What Kind of Gasoline Should I Use?

Your owner's manual should specify which octane gasoline your engine needs. If it doesn't, use the lowest octane that doesn't cause pinging. Pinging is a rattling noise from the engine (like shaking a glass jar full of uncooked popcorn). You will hear pinging when your foot is on the gas, and it is most pronounced when accelerating and going up hills. If your car does not require high-octane, premium gasoline, you are wasting your money. Octane is a measurement of how quickly gas burns and how well the gas prevents pinging. Pinging causes excessive wear on the engine and will shorten its life. Octane ratings are as follows: 87, regular (low octane); 89, mid; 91–93, premium (high octane).

How to Spend Less on Gasoline

· Drive at 55 mph (yeah, right).
· Use cruise control.
· Keep your tires properly inflated.
· Use the air conditioning only when you must.
· When stopped for more than a couple of minutes, shut off the engine rather than leave it running.
· Accelerate slowly rather than slamming on the gas pedal.

HOW TO TELL IF YOU HAVE A LEAK

OH YOU POOR DEAR

How You Can Tell If You Have a Fluid Leak

Low fluid level is the first sign that something is leaking. It is important to check the fluids yourself. Leaks never fix themselves, they only get worse. By the time the oil light comes on or your engine overheats, you may already have done serious and expensive damage to your car.

If a fluid is low a day or two after you've checked it and topped it off, there's a good chance you have a leak. This is why you need to check the fluids yourself: A mechanic may just top off the fluids and not mention that something was low. You won't find out there's a problem until you're stranded by repairs that will cost an arm and a leg.

If you suspect a leak, here's what to do: Flatten a cardboard box and leave it under your car overnight. Mark the spots where the two front tires are. Use rocks to keep the cardboard in place if you park your car outside. The next day you will know what color the leaking fluid is, the part of the engine from which it comes, and how much you are losing. If you notice that any liquid has either spilled or erupted inside the engine compartment or is leaking onto the ground, check all the fluids and add the right amount. Then, make an appointment with your mechanic to get the leak diagnosed and repaired. Some leaks can be fixed easily and cheaply, but others may require quite a bit of effort and money to repair.

Before and after a leak is repaired, keep an eye on where it was coming from. You don't need to be a mechanic, or even know what the parts of the engine are called, to find the source of a leak.

What Is a Gasket?

A gasket is a piece of material that sits between two metal parts to prevent leakage. When two pieces of metal are bolted together they don't always form a perfectly tight seal. Gaskets are used for sealing fluids (like gas, coolant, brake fluid, etc.) and air (like the compressed air inside the engine's cylinders or the exhaust gases).

Gaskets are often named for the part they seal. If there is a leak around the oil pan, for example, the oil-pan gasket is probably the problem. A seal is similar to a gasket in that it also prevents fluids from leaking. Some gaskets and seals are easy to replace, like the oil-drain plug gasket, which should be replaced every time the oil is changed. Other gaskets are very difficult to access, like the rear engine seal, because the transmission has to be removed first.

Checking Oil

Oil lubricates, cleans, and cools the engine. It is as important to the motor as blood is to our bodies. If there is no oil to lubricate the engine, the moving metal parts will "seize up," that is, melt together. If this happens, you will probably need a new engine. If the oil light on the dashboard comes on, stop driving right away! (See Chapter 2 for more on what to do when a dash light come on.)

Check your oil with the car parked on level ground and the engine off. It's best to check it when the engine is warm, but not hot. Never add oil without checking the dipstick first!

Pull the dipstick out and wipe it clean with a rag, and put it back in, making sure it is pushed all the way in. Pull it out again and see if you need to add any oil (see illustration on the next page). If the dipstick reads low, add a little oil at a time, checking each time. If it's not obvious where to add the oil, ask. Better you should feel silly asking an obvious question than damage your car by putting oil in the wrong hole. You can always add more oil, but if you put in too

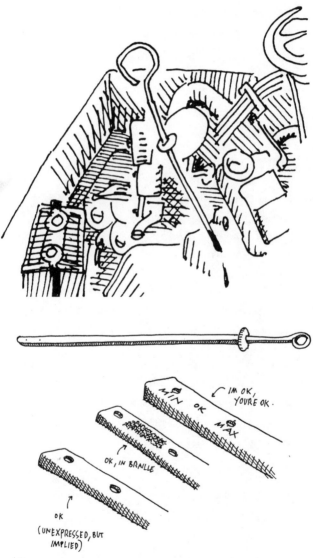

IM OK, YOU'RE OK.

MIN OK MAX

OK, IN BRAILLE

OK
(UNEXPRESSED, BUT IMPLIED)

much you can't get it out without a lot of trouble and some tools. Too much oil is bad for your engine, too. It can cause a gasket or seal to start leaking. Use a funnel so you don't spill. Don't forget to put the filler cap on and put the dipstick back in.

New oil that hasn't been in your engine very long is the color of honey. Used motor oil is dark brown or black. Motor oil is in the engine and can leak from a number of places. Some of the more typical oil leaks are: valve-cover gasket, oil-drain plug gasket, oil filter, oil-pan gasket, and front engine seal.

Types of Oil

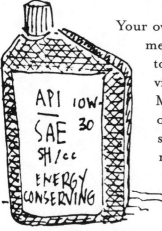

Your owner's manual recommends what type of oil to use. Oil is rated by viscosity, or thickness. Most cars use 10W-30 or 10W-40. The W stands for *winter*, and means that the oil can withstand both cold and hot temperatures. The lower the number, the thinner the oil. 90-weight oil is very thick, and 5 weight is very thin. This is what is meant by multigrade or multiviscosity oil. In the old days, people had to use different weights of oil depending on the season. Nowadays we can use one type of oil all year round.

Any good quality oil is SAE (Society of Automotive Engineers) Approved. Most of the known brand names are SAE approved and will also have the letters API (American Petroleum Institute) on the bottle. Check the label if you are using Jim Bob's Oil, or any brand you've never heard of.

Synthetic motor oil is a man-made oil, while regular oil is made from petroleum. The advantage of synthetic oil is that it takes longer to break down so it stays slippery longer and it cools better. Synthetic oil needs to be changed only every 7,500 miles. The downside is the oil and the filter still get dirty and can't clean themselves. Synthetic oil also costs two or three times as much as regular oil. You can also buy "synthetic blend" oil, which is a mix of synthetic and regular oil. Turbo-charged engines require oil that is specially rated for turbo engines.

Slick 50 is a one-time oil treatment purported to extend the life of your engine. A quart of Slick 50 costs nearly twenty dollars, but you use it only once. I'm usually not a big fan of "mechanic-in-a-can" solutions, but Slick 50 has been known to quiet noisy valve lifters. Whether it really makes a long-term difference is a matter of opinion.

Checking Coolant

Heat energy from burning gasoline is what powers the engine. Combustion engines create temperatures of nearly 3,000 degrees. The cooling system keeps the engine cool. The most important part of the cooling system is the coolant. If you are low on coolant, your engine will overheat. If your car starts running hot, you can easily check the coolant yourself. Never let the temperature gauge run into the red, unless you have a bunch of money you want to get rid of.

Do not take the radiator cap off on a car which is hot or overheating. Almost all cars, except much older models, have a coolant reservoir tank, or overflow bottle, which can be opened and filled at any time. It is a plastic container that holds extra coolant. This is where you check and add coolant. Look for a Low and Full line indicating how much coolant to add.

If you have to add coolant directly to the radiator let the engine cool down first, and use a few rags over the radiator cap as you slowly take it off. Radiators are pressurized, so be careful with a hot engine! On German cars the reservoir tank is also under pressure, so take care.

Coolant is a 50/50 mixture of antifreeze and water. It is important that your cooling system has this 50/50 mixture. Even if you live in a temperate climate you still need antifreeze: Straight water will rust your cooling system and cause problems later. Straight antifreeze doesn't cool as well as the 50/50 mixture, either.

Antifreeze is green (some newer products are using a reddish antifreeze), so if you see green liquid on the ground, there's a good chance you have a coolant leak. Coolant is slippery to the touch and sweet smelling. It can leak from the radiator, the radiator hoses, the water pump (driven by a belt at the front of the engine), or the freeze plugs, which are small round metal plugs on the side of the engine block. Coolant can also leak into your car, under the dash, if the heater core is leaking. The heater core uses the coolant that is warmed up by the engine to heat the car when you put the heat on.

Don't leave spilled antifreeze lying around. It is poisonous; dogs and cats will drink it. Leaks that don't get fixed will eventually leave permanent stains on your garage floor or driveway. You can absorb and sweep up large leaks or spills

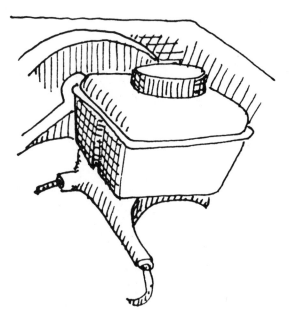

BRAKE MASTER CYLINDER.

with kitty litter or rice hull ash (available at auto parts stores). Floor stains are best removed with an industrial-strength floor cleaner.

Checking Brake Fluid

Cars use a hydraulic system to power the brakes. This means that a fluid is squished to create greater force than your foot can. The pressure in the brake lines is upwards of 1,600 pounds per square inch. The tiniest leak can cause brake failure. This is why it's important to check the brake fluid when you check the other fluids. You should also have all the brakes and the brake lines checked at least once a year.

The brake reservoir is usually toward the rear of the engine compartment, on the right side as you are facing the front of your car. Imagine where your brake pedal would end up if it continued through the floorboard to the engine compartment. The brake reservoir is a part of your brake master cylinder.

There may or may not be a Full line marked on the reservoir, and some of the reservoirs are clear so you can see through them. Always add DOT (Department of Transportation) 3 or 4 brake fluid. Do not fill to the very top, only to the Full line. Take care not to spill brake fluid on the car's paint, as it is corrosive.

Brake fluid is tan or clear colored. It is greasy and slippery to the touch. It can leak from the master cylinder (below the brake reservoir where you add fluid), any of the brake hoses that bring fluid to all four brakes, or at any of the brakes at each wheel. If the brake master cylinder is leaking badly enough it will sometimes leak into the car, behind the brake pedal.

If you have to add brake fluid frequently, or you suspect there is a leak in the brake hydraulic system, get it checked out right away. If you don't deal with a brake fluid leak, eventually all the brake fluid will leak out. How long this will take depends on the size of the leak. Without brake fluid, you will have great difficulty stopping your car. Losing your brakes is exciting, but not recommended.

Checking Windshield-Washer Fluid

Windshield-washer fluid may seem like an unnecessary extra, as far as fluids go, but in reality it can be a lifesaver. Imagine driving down the highway in a rainstorm, and a large truck splashes your entire windshield with a sheet of mud and dirt. Your vision becomes completely obstructed and you crash.

Windshield-washer fluid is detergent for cleaning your windshield; it also contains antifreeze to prevent it from freezing when it hits your windshield. It is blue in color. Don't use radiator antifreeze or dish soap instead of windshield-washer fluid. Antifreeze will make the glass greasy, and dish soap is too bubbly, and it will not keep the water from freezing. Also, some nerd probably spent hours in a laboratory coming up with the best thing for cleaning bugs off glass. Give him a break.

Windshield-washer fluid usually comes in concentrated form, and you have to add water. You can also buy it premixed, but it will take up a lot of space in the trunk Don't worry about getting the ratio of water to concentrate exact; just make it blue, you'll be fine.

Checking Automatic-Transmission Fluid (ATF)

ATF should be checked regularly in cars with automatic transmissions. A transmission with low ATF will not shift smoothly. If all the fluid leaks out, the engine will run but the car won't go. You can seriously damage the transmission by driving your car without enough ATF.

Your car has a second dipstick that looks like the oil dipstick. This dipstick goes into the transmission instead of into the engine block. The transmission bolts to the back of the engine. The belts are always at the front of the engine, so the transmission and the dipstick for checking the transmission will be at the opposite end of where the belts are.

Check the transmission fluid with the car idling, in park or neutral (some cars require the engine to be off—check your owner's manual). Make sure you are parked on level ground. Check the dipstick the same way you would if you were checking oil: Pull it out, wipe it off, put it back in, then check the level on the stick when you pull it out the second time.

Some cars require you to check the ATF when the car is warmed up, others will give two different marks for hot or cold. Use a funnel to add ATF, because you will add it into that little hole that you pull the dipstick out of. Yeah, that little, tiny hole. Add only a little at a time (less than half a quart), and keep checking so you don't overfill.

Automatic-transmission fluid is red and oily. It can leak from the transmission, which is bolted to the back of the engine (the front of your engine is where the belts are) or the transmission fluid cooling lines, which go from the transmission to the radiator.

There are two types of automatic-transmission fluid: Dexron (Mercron) or Type F. Your owner's manual will specify which type your car requires. There are three types of Dexron ATF: Dexron, Dexron II, and Dexron III. If your transmission requires Dexron III you cannot use the lower numbered Dexron ATF.

Checking Clutch Fluid

Clutch fluid! What's that? There really is no such thing as "clutch fluid," so don't go into a parts store and ask to buy a bottle. Many manual transmissions use a fluid in the clutch system—brake fluid. The clutch hydraulic system is a completely separate system from the brakes, but it uses the same fluid.

Cars with manual transmissions have either a clutch cable or a hydraulic clutch system. Cars with a clutch cable do not use any fluid. If your car has two reservoirs that look alike, one is the brake reservoir, the other is the clutch reservoir. The clutch reservoir (or clutch master cylinder) is located near the brake fluid reservoir. Follow the clutch pedal straight through to the engine compartment and you'll find it to the far right, as you face the engine.

Check the hydraulic clutch fluid when you check the other fluids. This reservoir looks similar to the brake reservoir but is slightly smaller. Add brake fluid. Fill it to the upper mark.

If there is no fluid in the clutch master cylinder, your car will start and idle but it will not go. You may not be able to put it in gear, and the clutch pedal will feel floppy and weak.

Clutch hydraulics can leak from the clutch master cylinder (where you check and add fluid) and from the clutch slave cylinder, which is bolted to the outside of the transmission. There are also lines that connect these two parts that can leak. The clutch master cylinder is usually fairly small, so a leak can empty it quite quickly. The clutch master cylinder can also leak into the car, behind the clutch pedal.

Checking Power-Steering Fluid

If you don't have power steering, you won't have to check this fluid. If you can parallel park while eating an ice cream cone, you have power steering.

A leak can cause the power-steering pump to run dry, which will damage it. New power-steering pumps are expensive, so check this fluid regularly.

Where you add power-steering fluid may be in different places on different model cars, but it's usually near the power-steering pump, which is driven by a belt. Locate the belts, then find a device that is belt driven and has a reservoir on top of it. If you are lucky, it's labeled.

Remove the cap: It will have a small dipstick attached to it. Check the fluid level with the dipstick. Some power-steering reservoirs are clear and do not have a dipstick, so you don't have to take the cap off to see the fluid level. If the reservoir is not on the power-steering pump, there will be hoses coming from the pump to the reservoir.

Use the approved fluid for your car—some are designed just for American cars or just for Japanese cars. Check the label on the bottle. The wrong kind of fluid will eat the seals in the pump or steering rack and cause leaks.

Power-steering fluid is yellowish or clear colored. Some cars use ATF in the power-steering system. Check your owner's manual. It can leak from the power-steering pump, the pump hoses, or under the car, from the power-steering rack. Some cars use Dexron ATF in the power-steering system instead of power-steering fluid. Don't assume this will work in your car unless it clearly says so in the owner's manual.

Fluids You Can't Easily Check Yourself (But Which Still Need Regular Checking)

I don't want to discourage anyone from working on her own car, but checking the following fluids involves tools and/or jacking up the car. You can ask to have these fluids checked when you get an oil change, so it's not a big deal.

Manual-Transmission-Gear Oil

This oil keeps the gears in the transmission lubricated. Many manual transmissions use 90-weight gear oil, but some use ATF or motor oil. Check the owner's manual under "fluid specifications." The manual-transmission oil is not easy to check because you have to check it from underneath the car and it has to be pumped in with a special pump; you can't just fill it with a funnel. You may want to spend the extra money and put synthetic gear oil in the manual transmission. Synthetic oil keeps its lubricating properties longer than regular oil.

Differential-Gear Oil

Only cars with real-wheel drive have a differential. The differential is a set of gears that allow the two back wheels to spin at the same speed when the car is turning. These gears are lubricated with 90-weight gear oil. Like the manual transmission, the differential-gear oil has to be pumped in, and it can't be checked without the right tool.

90-weight gear oil is honey colored or dark, depending on age. Gear oil is thicker than motor oil, and is used in the transmission and in the differential (the gears at the back of your car, part of the "rear end," if you have a rear-wheel drive vehicle). It has a more pungent odor than motor oil.

Battery Electrolyte

The liquid chemical in the battery is called battery acid, or electrolyte. The electrolyte can be replenished with distilled water. Some batteries are sealed and cannot be opened to add water. The battery-fluid level should be checked when the battery is serviced. Servicing a battery includes cleaning the terminal ends, adding water, and testing the battery for proper electrical output. Some shops include this in a tune-up. If not, request a battery service, especially if you notice the battery terminals are fuzzy with white or blue-green corrosion.

Battery acid is highly corrosive and can burn skin and clothing. A battery that is low on fluid will not be able to hold a charge, and your car will crank slowly or not at all (see Chapter 6 on batteries and jump-starting).

Chapter 5

Tires, and How to Change a Tire Like a Pro

How to Tell if You Need New Tires

Your tires are the only part of the car that touches the ground. A smooth ride, good handling, and your personal safety depend on tires that are in good condition. How often you need new tires will depend on your driving habits. Most people need new tires every three to five years. Don't skimp when it comes to tires. A blowout at high speeds can be a life-threatening situation!

Make a point of periodically checking the tire tread on all four tires. The penny method, while not entirely accurate, is an easy way to make a preliminary check of the depth of your tire tread. Stick a penny into the groove; if you can see the top of Lincoln's head, it's probably time for new tires. Better yet, purchase a tread depth gauge (about $15) for an easy and more accurate way to check tire wear. Tires don't always wear evenly, so check the thinnest or most worn part of the tire. If you are unsure whether you need new tires, ask your mechanic. But ask at a shop that doesn't sell tires.

Under normal conditions, tires wear fairly evenly. Uneven tire wear is an indication of improper tire inflation or a wheel-alignment problem. Under inflation will create thin tread on both the inner and outer sides of the tire. Over inflation creates a wear pattern along the middle of the tire. Tread wear on either the inside or the outside of the tire is a sign of a car out of an alignment. Replacing tires that are worn due to an alignment problem is a waste of money if you don't get an alignment right after putting the new tires on.

Tires can also wear out as a result of bad shock absorbers or struts. The tires become scalloped, creating a rough ride and road noise. Run your hand along the tread part of the tire. If it feels bumpy or uneven, it's time for new tires, even if the tread is still deep. Before purchasing new tires see about replacing the shocks or struts that caused this problem in the first place.

Checking Tire Pressure

You cannot check your tire pressure just by looking at the tires, or even by kicking them. You must use a tire pressure gauge. Cheap tire gauges are good to have in a pinch, but they are often inaccurate. Find a garage that has an air hose with a good gauge attached to it or spring for the extra money to buy a good gauge that you can

UNDERINFLATION
CAUSES TIRES TO WEAR
ALONG BOTH OUTER
EDGES.

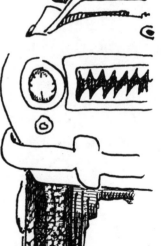

OVERINFLATION
CAUSES TIRES TO WEAR
DOWN THE MIDDLE.

OUT OF ALIGNMENT CAUSES TIRES TO WEAR ALONG ONE SIDE OR THE OTHER.

keep in your glove compartment (about $20).

Look for a label on the doorjamb of the driver's side to find the recommended tire pressure. Your tires will also have a tire pressure rating, although this usually indicates only the maximum tire pressure. Tires should be filled to maximum pressure only when you are hauling everything you own and your grandmother in the car. If you can't find any stickers indicating the correct tire pressure, a good rule of thumb is to keep them between 28 and 32 psi (pounds per square inch). The owner's manual will also supply you with the correct tire pressure. You'll get better gas mileage (but a bumpier ride) if you fill the tires to the higher recommended pressure.

Check the tire pressure when the car is cold, and hasn't been driven for a few hours. Air expands when it gets hot, so you will get an

NERD
GAUGE

incorrect reading if you add air to a tire that's been on the road for a while.

Find the valve stem on the tire. It may have a little plastic cap that unscrews. Take the cap off and press the bulbous end of the gauge firmly into the valve. If you hear a *whooshing* noise, you are letting air out: Either you aren't pressing firmly enough into the valve or the gauge is at an angle that is allowing air to seep past it. When you have the gauge pressed against the valve you should get a reading.

To add air you will need to go to a gas station. Some places charge twenty-five cents for compressed air; but don't worry, the machine stays on long enough to fill all four tires. When adding air, push the air hose into the valve firmly until you don't hear any *whooshing* noise. Then press the lever on the handle to put air in. Check the pressure after thirty seconds or so to see how much air has gone in. Repeat until you get to the desired psi.

If you put too much air in, it's very easy to take it out. In the middle of the valve stem hole is a tiny metal rod; push it with your fingernail or the tip of a pencil and you'll hear that *whooshing* noise again, telling you that air is coming out. Too much air in your tires will wear the tread prematurely, give you a bumpy ride, and increase your chances of getting a blowout or flat.

Eight cars out of ten have a spare tire in the trunk that is flat, rendering it completely useless in the event of a flat tire on the road. Don't forget to put air in the spare tire! Economy cars have "temporary" spare tires, which are smaller so they can fit in the trunk. These tires are also labeled on the side wall, and should be filled to 60 psi. You can't drive very far or fast with a temporary spare, but it will get you to the next service station.

Buying New Tires

Whenever possible, buy tires in pairs (two front tires or two rear tires). Obviously, if you must replace a damaged tire and the other of the pair is still in good shape, it is acceptable to replace only one. New tires should always be the same size as the other tires on the car. You can get different size tires when replacing all four tires, provided the size you are changing to is correct for your car. All tire shops have a reference manual for which size tires are suitable for your particular car. Using the largest recommended tire size gives better wear, a better ride and handling, and increased gas mileage.

Mounting and balancing tires is part of purchasing new tires. Mounting a tire means the tire is put onto the wheel rim. A tire without a rim is good for only one thing: hanging on a tree to make a swing. Mechanics use a machine just for the purpose of mounting tires to rims; it's not something you can do yourself.

Tire Size: What the Numbers on Your Tires Mean

P 185 75 R 14

P: passenger car
185: tire width in millimeters
75: the ratio of the tire width to the tire height (the lower the number, the wider the tire looks)
R: radial (all tires are now radial, old cars will have a B, for bias ply)
14: the rim diameter

Tire Grades

1. **90–150:** tread wear; a tire graded 150 should last about 45,000 miles.
2. **A, B, or C:** Traction and temperature resistance A has the greatest traction and withstands the highest temperatures.

Wheel Balancing

A tire and its rim must be evenly weighted or you will experience a shimmy, or vibration. Front wheels that need balancing will create a vibration you feel in the steering wheel. Rear wheels out of balance make the seat underneath you vibrate

slightly. You will feel this vibration only at certain speeds, not all the time. For instance, say you feel a vibration only when you're driving between 55 and 60 miles per hour. There is a good chance one or more of your wheels are out of balance. A vibration that occurs all the time, or during low speeds, is an entirely different problem. Make an appointment to get a diagnosis.

Wheel balancing is fairly inexpensive (about ten dollars a tire), so there's no reason to put it off. A wheel-balancing machine weighs the tire and checks for symmetry, and then small lead weights are attached to the rim to create even weight all around.

Brand-new tires always get balanced before they are put on your car. Wheels go out of balance as they age and the weight in the tire shifts, or if you knock a weight off the rim while parking.

Wheel Alignment

A car that is correctly aligned will drive down the road in a straight line without drifting or pulling to one side. Cars will go out of alignment from hitting bumps and curbs, or as a result of an accident, even a minor fender-bender. All cars will need an alignment at one time or another.

A wheel alignment isn't especially costly, but it pays to have it done if you notice your car pulling to one side. Misaligned wheels will eventually cause noticeable tire wear, and you will end up wearing your tires prematurely.

To test if your car needs an alignment, rest your hands gently on the steering wheel. See if it travels in a straight line. Try this on several different roads to account for wind and curves in the road. If your car consistently drifts to one side, first check the tire pressure—uneven tire

pressure can cause your car to pull. If it still pulls, make an appointment to have the wheels aligned. Some cars have alignment adjustments for all four wheels, and others can have only the front wheels aligned.

How to Change a Tire Like a Pro

Modern-day tires are very sturdy, and you may only get a flat tire once or twice in a lifetime, but changing a tire is so easy there's no reason not to learn. AAA and other road services can change a flat tire for you, but if there's no phone for miles, they are of little help. Roadside service can also take up to an hour to reach you, and it

International signal for HELP.

takes less than ten minutes to change a tire. You can minimize (but not eliminate) the chances of getting a flat tire by keeping your tires properly inflated, replacing tires when the tread is worn, and avoiding driving over glass and nails.

OK, first things first. Here are some easy-to-remember precautions for dealing with a flat tire.

- Remain calm. Don't panic and don't slam on the brakes. Using the turn signal and then the hazard lights, slowly pull off the road.

- Park on a firm shoulder, as far from the traffic as is safely possible. Do not pull over on a bridge, under or on an overpass, or near a curve in the road. Try to park on level ground.

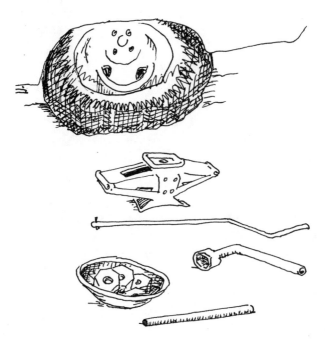

- Turn off the ignition and leave the hazard lights on. Set the parking brake and put the car in gear. Passengers should either get out of the car or leave their seat belts on.

- Open the hood of the car to indicate that you are having car troubles. If you have flares or reflector triangles, use them.

Your owner's manual has instructions on how to change a tire and how your jack works, but in case you don't have your owner's manual with you, or the instructions are too brief, here's a detailed step-by-step plan of action. Take a deep breath and let's go. This is going to be a cinch.

1. Make sure you have everything you need to change a flat: a spare tire (with air in it), a jack and all its parts, and a lugnut wrench. Sometimes you will have to turn the jack by hand to get it out of the trunk; it may be purposefully wedged into a small compartment to keep it from moving around and to save space. I have had many students swear they don't have a jack in their car, only to find it cleverly hidden under the trunk mat or behind a plastic cover on the side of the trunk. Subarus keep the spare tire in the engine compartment, and pickup trucks have a spare under the bed of the truck. To lower a spare tire out from under a pickup truck, there should be a long rod in the engine compartment, alongside the hood prop.

2. To prevent the car from rolling, use a rock or any heavy object to block the wheel diagonally across from the wheel you are changing.

3. On cars with hubcaps, remove the hubcaps with a screwdriver. Some lugnut wrenches have a chiseled end for this purpose.

4. First, loosen the lugnuts (the four or five nuts that hold the tire on). Yes—before you jack up the car! Just loosen them, don't remove them yet. If you jack up the car first the tire will spin and you won't be able to get the nuts off. Remember, "lefty-loosy, righty-tighty." This means that to loosen a nut or bolt turn it counterclockwise, and to tighten it turn it clockwise. Take a moment to make sure you are turning the nut the correct way

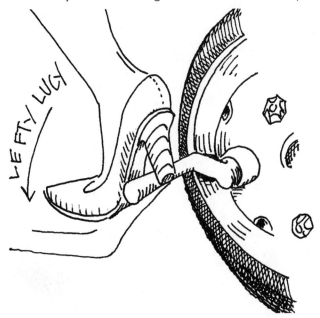

LEFTY LUCY

before beginning. Leverage is everything when it comes to removing lugnuts. It's always smart to carry a "breaker bar," which is a fancy name for any pipe about two feet long, hollow, and wide enough to fit over the lugnut wrench. Trying to loosen a lugnut with a wrench that is one foot long and one that is three feet long is the difference between hurting your back or not (or sometimes being able to remove the lugnuts at all!). Position the lugnut wrench so you are pulling up on it, rather than pushing. You will have more torque this way and won't hit your knuckles on the ground when the nut loosens.

TIRE AND LUGNUTS.

If you still can't loosen the nut, position the wrench so you can use your feet or stand on the end of it. This is perfectly acceptable; don't worry about looking dorky.

Put the lugnuts in your pocket or someplace obvious so you don't lose them or kick them away by accident.

5. Familiarize yourself with how your jack goes up and down before trying to jack up the car. If you don't have a jack, take a trip to the local junkyard and see if you can pick one up cheap. Some jacks have two or three pieces, so make sure you have all the parts. If you are reading this in your armchair at home, pick a time to learn how your jack works, so when you do get a flat you

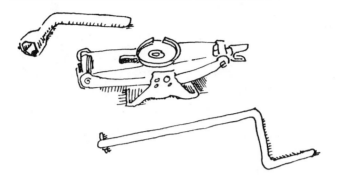

already know where the jack is and how it works. If you are standing on the side of the road reading this, well, it's going to be trial by fire, isn't it?

6. Position the jack under the car (see illustration). Most cars have four reinforced areas, on the body near each tire, along a rim that runs the length of the car. This is where the top of your jack fits. Some cars (Volvos and BMWs, for example), have a special jack that fits into a notch (again, there are four of them) designed just for jacking up the car.

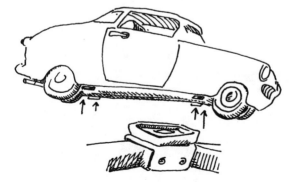

JACK POSITION.

American cars from the '60s and '70s use bumper jacks, which hook on to the front or rear bumper. Don't use a bumper jack on a modern car—the bumper is not strong enough to hold the weight of the car. Once you have the jack in place, slowly start jacking up the car. Remarkable, isn't it? You can lift a car all by yourself. Jack the car up high enough to be able to put on the new tire. Remember, the old tire is flat, so leave more room for the full tire.

7. Take the flat tire off and put the spare tire on. If you are confused about which way the tire goes on, just look for the valve stem, where the air goes in. The valve stem will always be facing out.

8. Put the lugnuts on by hand, taking care that they go on smoothly and are not cross threaded. Then tighten the lugnuts in a crisscross or star

pattern using the wrench. The crisscross pattern ensures that the tire is flush against the hub.

10. Jack the car down and remove the jack from under the car.

11. **Very important**: Tighten the lugnuts with the wrench a second time, as tight as you can.

Real Spare Tire vs. Temporary Spare

Many cars have temporary spare tires, which are smaller and can be used only to travel short distances at slower speeds (under 55 mph). You can tell a temporary spare not only by its size but also because it says "temporary" on the side, and also "fill to 60 psi." Regular tires usually need 28 to 32 psi of air. A temporary spare is fine in a pinch. It will get you to the nearest service sta-

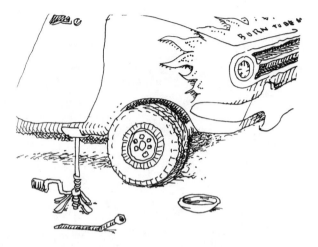

tion, where you can have your tire repaired or replaced. But if your trunk is large enough, it's not a bad idea to get a real spare tire. Next time you buy new tires, ask for the best of the old ones back (unless they are all very bald). Go to a junk-yard and buy a rim for your particular car, and have the old tire mounted on the rim. You now have a real spare. If you get a flat tire, you can use this spare and won't have to fix or replace the flat tire immediately. You can wait a day or two or until it is convenient to deal with it.

Tire Maintenance

I. Check the tire pressure regularly. Keep the tires filled to the proper specifications.

2. Get an alignment if you notice the car drifts consistently in one direction. (Check the tire pressure first to make sure uneven tire pressure isn't causing the pull.) Also have your car aligned after any accident, even a minor one.

3. Balance the wheels if you notice a vibration at higher speeds.

4. Rotate your tires once a year.

5. Worn suspension (shock absorbers or struts) will cause tires to scallop, or wear unevenly. The result is road noise like a deep hum at higher speeds and a rough ride.

6. Try not to force the side of the tires up against the curb when parallel parking.

Chapter 6

Jump-Starting with Ease and Confidence

How to Tell If You Need a Jump-Start

There is only one problem a jump start will fix: a dead or weak battery. So before you go digging through the trunk for jumper cables, verify that the problem is with your battery. Turn the key to the On position and turn the windshield wipers on. Do they move at normal speed? If your wipers and all your accessories work, the problem is probably not with your battery and jump-starting is not going to help you.

If the engine doesn't crank, check these things first:
- Is the transmission in neutral?
- Is the clutch pedal depressed?
- Is your seatbelt belt on?

If the wipers and other accessories do not work, or work very slowly, there's a good chance the problem is a low or dead battery. A low battery may have enough juice to operate the accessories (usually slowly) but not enough to crank the starter motor and start the car.

First, see if you left the lights on or a door ajar. If so, all you need is a jump start and you're on your way. If the lights weren't left on you will want to find out why your battery was dead later. Either you need a new battery or there is a problem with your charging system. A mechanic can check these things for you.

Before jump-starting, visually inspect the connections at the battery. Are they fuzzy with bluish white corrosion? Enough corrosion will keep your car from starting, with symptoms identical to a dead battery. Are the connections tight? You shouldn't be able to turn the battery cable ends on the battery post. A loose connection can also prevent your car from cranking and starting. If a battery cable end is loose, and you don't have a wrench to tighten it, sometimes just turning it a little bit will be enough to create a better connection so you can start your car. If you can, follow the positive battery cable to the starter and check that the connection at the starter is also tight.

How to Jump-Start Your Car Safely

Once you've determined that a loose connection is not the culprit, prop open the hood and get your jumper cables out. Now, stand on the side of the road and hold the cables up in the air. This is the universal sign for "Help, my car needs a jump start." Without your own set of jumper cables it is often difficult to get people to stop. If you are standing on the side of the road waving your arms, they have no idea what you want. Displaying jumper cables is also a good way to get someone to stop even if you don't need a jump.

Sometimes people will try to avoid helping you by claiming that their little Toyota doesn't have a battery powerful enough to jump-start your Cadillac. This is just an excuse for laziness. Unless you have a ten-ton dump truck, there's no reason why they can't help you jump-start your car.

Once you've found someone to give you a jump-start, the first step is to position the two cars so that the jumper cables can reach from

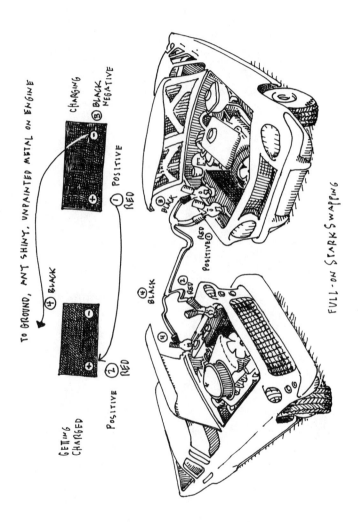

battery to battery. Look under the hoods first and check which side of the engine compartment the batteries sit in. Make sure the cars are not touching, as this can damage the electrical equipment. Double-check the symbols + and - or Pos and Neg on the battery and then attach the cables to the battery. Just because a battery cable is red, do not assume it is the positive cable: Always double-check by looking for the + and - or the words Pos and Neg. Follow the order of connection as illustrated below. It is crucial that you pay close attention, because putting the jumper cables on backward (called reversing the polarity) can cause expensive and serious damage to the alternator and possibly the car's main computer.

The "ground" connection on the dead car means you will attach the negative jumper cable to an engine ground. Any part of the engine (not the body) that is metal, unpainted, and sturdy looking will make a good ground. You may have to fiddle with the cable ends a couple of times to get a good connection. Don't freak out if there are some small sparks when hooking up the jumper cables—this is norml and won't hurt you. As my teacher in trade school used to say, it's not getting shocked by 12 volts that hurts, it's when you jump up in surprise and bang your head on the hood.

Once you have attached everything, start the engine with the good battery, then start the engine with the dead battery. If the engine still won't start, you probably don't have a good connection. Fiddle with the jumper cable ends until you can get the dead car to crank.

Disconnect the cables with both cars running. Take the cables off in the opposite way you put them on (see illustration on page 77). Once your car starts, run it for at least 15 to 20 minutes before turning it off. This allows time for the alternator to recharge the battery. The alternator charges the battery only when the engine is on. If the reason the battery is dead is because the charging system is not working, then you will not be able to keep your car running once you remove the jumper cables. If the alternator quits charging or the alternator belt is loose, the battery light on your dash should light up while you are driving long before your battery is dead.

Chapter 7

Maintenance and Repairs: What to Do and When to Do It

What Is Preventive Maintenance? Why Bother?

It would be nice if all you ever had to do was put gas in the your car and drive. Unfortunately, all cars needs a little more attention than that. As technology improves, cars need less maintenance than they did twenty or thirty years ago, but even new cars still need regular attention.

Maintenance means replacing parts before they break. More than half the cars that get towed in for repairs have problems that could have been prevented with regular maintenance. All cars need regular servicing. Even a brand new, so-called "self-tuning" engine needs observation and periodic maintenance. **Maintenance includes more than just tune-ups and oil changes**. You can avoid costly surprises if you set up a schedule for your car and keep track of what it needs.

If the manufacturer's recommendations suggest a tune-up (sometimes included under the title "major service") every 30,000 miles, it doesn't mean your car will stop working at exactly that time. If you need to wait a few extra thousand miles it won't harm your car. But remember, you can't make up for lost time when it comes to oil changes, so do them regularly! Also, ignoring your brakes and tires is dangerous, so don't wait if there's a problem there.

Preventive maintenance will save you money in the long run. It will also decrease the chances of getting stuck on the side of the road or having an accident.

Understanding the Owner's Manual

To find out what your car needs start with the owner's manual. If you don't have the owner's manual, you can buy one at the local dealer. It's not very expensive and you'll be glad to have it. Read through the owner's manual. You'll probably find out things about your car you never knew, even if you've owned it for years.

Occasionally the manufacturer will leave certain things out of the recommended service schedule. This is not an oversight. New cars get rated according to a number of criteria—driveability, looks, comfort, as well as operating costs. The manufacturer may leave out important maintenance items so the car will rate better and get high recommendations. If your owner's manual omits, for example, changing the fuel filter, this doesn't mean that it doesn't ever need to be changed.

Creating a Personalized Maintenance Schedule

Different cars require different maintenance schedules. Unfortunately, there isn't one list that can be applied to all cars. The maintenance schedule for your car and your neighbor's car may be totally different. As technology improves, service intervals on newer cars are further apart and less maintenance is needed. To create your own personalized maintenance schedule, use a combination of your owner's manual and the recommended service suggested on the following pages. The chart in your owner's manual can be a little hard to decipher, so you may want to sit down and make a list you can easily refer to.

Look through your old service records and find out what's been done and what you can expect to pay in the future. Keep a small spiral notepad in the glove compartment and write down the date, mileage, and what repairs were made whenever you bring your car to the shop. Keep all the receipts and service records in one place, ideally a large manila envelope or a sturdy folder.

Be sure to bring all the old repair orders with you when you take your car in to the shop; when diagnosing, mechanics often want to see what was done to the car in the past. Just like a medical doctor, auto mechanics work better with a good history of the patient. Maintaining good records about your car's history will also make it easier to sell, if and when that time comes.

The average American drives 15,000 miles a year. The recommended maintenance suggested in this book should be read as "every year, or 15,000 miles, whichever comes first." Tailor your maintenance schedule to your particular driving habits. If you drive only 5,000 miles a year, you may be spending more money on maintenance than you need to.

The Most Important Maintenance: Changing the Oil

The most important maintenance you can do to extend your car's life is to change the oil. The oil lubricates the moving metal parts inside the engine. It is as important to your engine as blood is to our bodies. The difference between an engine that needs rebuilding at 100,000 miles and one that keeps kicking for years is how often the oil was changed.

Change the oil and the oil filter every 3,000 miles. If you have trouble remembering this, try to change the oil every season: spring, summer, winter, and fall. Never mind that your manual recommends oil changes every 7,500 miles. Car manufacturers in the U.S. are required by law to provide an oil change schedule so consumers can include maintenance costs in comparison shopping. But if you read the owner's manual carefully you can usually find a self-protective disclaimer stating that city driving is considered severe use, and recommending more frequent oil changes. If you put very few miles on your car each year, change the oil every six months. The oil still gets contaminated by moisture and dust over time.

The inexpensive quick-oil-change chains give the best deal. An oil change is not a complicated procedure, so you don't have to go to the dealer or a specialized shop. Just don't let them sell you an air filter every time you get an oil change. You don't need a new air filter more than once a year, unless you drive on dusty roads every day.

Oil changes are often advertised as a combination lube and oil change. Lubricating the front end is when a mechanic uses a grease gun to squirt grease into various components of your front end: ball joints, tie-rod ends, steering linkage, etc. Many later model cars have sealed

lube fittings. If your car's front end has sealed fittings, you do not need to have them lubed. Some shops will charge extra for a lube when all they are doing is spraying a little WD-40 on the door hinges!

Brakes and tires are also a top priority when it comes to maintenance. Worn tires or brakes that are not working properly are a safety hazard. Don't wait until the last minute to deal with your brakes or get new tires.

Monthly Maintenance Checklist

☑ Check and fill the engine oil.

☑ Check and fill the coolant.

☑ Check and fill the brake fluid.

☑ Check and fill the automatic-transmission or clutch fluid.

☑ Check and fill the windshield-washer reservoir.

☑ Check and fill the power-steering fluid (if applicable).

☑ Check the tire pressure and the spare tire.

☑ Visually check for any fluid leaks on the engine or on the ground.

These are all things you can and should check yourself!

Yearly Maintenance (or Every 15,000 Miles) Checklist

1. Replace the air filter and the fuel filter. Older cars (pre-1980) require a thorough tune-up once a year, or every 15,000 miles. Newer cars can go 30,000 miles or more between tune-ups. Check your owner's manual and read the following chapter on tune-ups.

2. Check the brakes once a year, whether you hear noise or not. When the brakes are checked the rear drum brakes should also be adjusted if they are not the self-adjusting type. Cars with four-wheel disk brakes have no adjustment, although you can get the parking brake adjusted. If you do a lot of city driving or drive in a hilly or mountainous area, get the brakes checked every six months.

3. Rotate the tires (this is currently a matter of opinion and some controversy: many mechanics claim that rotating tires causes radial tires to wear faster during break-in).

4. Check all the belts and hoses and replace if needed.

5. Check and adjust the clutch (stick-shift cars only). There should be about one half inch of "free play," or slack, at the clutch pedal. Driving your car with a clutch pedal that needs an adjustment will wear the clutch prematurely. Some cars have self-adjusting clutches. See your owner's manual or ask your mechanic.

6. Check the transmission-gear oil (stick-shift cars). You cannot do this yourself, because the car has to be jacked up or on a lift and the gear oil gets pumped in.

7. On front-wheel-drive cars, **check the CV boots** when the brakes are checked. CV stands for constant velocity. The CV boots are rubber boots that keep the CV joints packed in grease. If the boot rips, the grease will come out and the joint will be damaged. A ripped CV boot can cause joint damage in less than a week. It is cheaper to replace a torn CV boot than to replace the CV joint or the entire axle. If you are told you have a torn CV boot, ask your mechanic to show you. This is something that you can easily verify yourself.

8. Check the differential-gear oil (rear-wheel drive only). You cannot do this yourself, because the car has to be jacked up or put on a lift and the gear oil gets pumped in.

9. Lubricate the front end (newer cars have sealed fittings and cannot be lubed). Lubing the front end employs the use of a special grease gun. It only takes a few minutes, but the car usually must be jacked up or on a lift.

10. Lubricate the door, hood, and trunk

hinges. Nothing fancy here, it only means using WD-40 or some other spray lubricant on all the car's hinges to keep them squeak free.

What do front- and rear-wheel drive mean?

Front-wheel drive means the power from the engine drives the front wheels; rear-wheel drive means the power goes to the rear wheels. Only front-wheel drive cars have CV joints and Boots, two on the left axle and two on the right axle. A rear-wheel drive car has a differential in the back of the car, and "universal joints" on the driveshaft.

Winterizing Your Car (Every Winter)

Winter can be an especially hard time on your car. A car that runs just fine in the fall may have trouble starting and running smoothly once the first cold spell hits. Keeping your car tuned up and winterizing it every autumn can avert getting stuck in the cold.

* **Radiator**: Flush the cooling system and replace the coolant (50/50 mixture of antifreeze and water) every two years, or every autumn if you live in a harsh climate.
* **Windshield-wiper blades**: Replace once a year.

❋ **Windshield-wiper fluid**: Keep windshield-wiper reservoir filled with water *and* windshield-wiper detergent. Use the blue stuff. Do not use radiator antifreeze or dish soap for the windshield washer! Keep an ice scraper in the car.

❋ **Gas**: Keep the tank as full as possible to avoid moisture that can freeze in the gas lines.

❋ **Battery**: Make sure the battery is in good condition. Have it load tested (to see how well it can hold a charge) and serviced. Servicing a battery includes cleaning the battery terminals and adding water to the battery. Buy a new battery if your present one is more than four years old.

❋ **Tires**: Make sure the tires are in good condition and have the proper amount of air in them. If you live or vacation in snow country, keep chains in the trunk. Practice putting them on before you have to do it in a raging blizzard. Check the spare and the jack, too. Put air in the spare tire.

❋ Check all the **lights**, and the **heater** and **defroster**.

❋ If you live or vacation in mountain or snow country, carry a **winter emergency kit**. This can include blankets, extra gloves and boots, a small shovel, an ice scraper, and a flashlight. For getting stuck in the snow or ice, kitty litter or sand under the tires is good for traction.

Two-Year (or Every 30,000 Miles) Maintenance Checklist

1. Most manufacturers suggest a **tune-up** (or "major service") every 30,000 miles. Check your owner's manual and read the chapter on tune-ups.

2. A **transmission service** should be done every two years or 30,000 miles on cars with automatic transmissions. A "tranny service" includes changing the ATF and replacing the transmission pan gasket and the filter in the transmission.

3. Flush the cooling system and change the coolant every two years. People who live in cold climates need to do this every autumn. On older cars do not use any sort of "fast flush" cleaner. It sometimes causes leaks as the corrosion it is meant to flush out is what's sealing potential holes in the radiator.

4. Flush the brake system and replace the brake fluid. To save some money, ask for this to be done when you get a brake job.

5. Check the condition of your **tires and exhaust system**.

6. Wheel alignment: It's a good idea to get a wheel alignment every couple of years. If you've been in an accident, even a small fender bender, you should definitely get an alignment. Also get an alignment if your tires show uneven wear or your cars pulls to one direction. Some cars

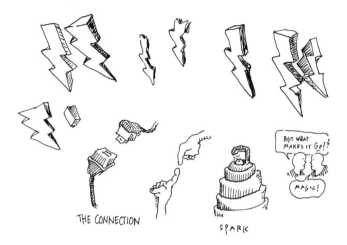

THE CONNECTION

SPARK

BUT WHAT MAKES IT Go!?

MAGIC!

require four-wheel alignments, on others only the front end can be aligned.

Four-Year (or Every 60,000 Miles) Maintenance Checklist

I. Replace the **timing belt** (if applicable) and all the other drive belts. Replacing the timing belt isn't cheap, but if you don't do it you may face more expensive repairs when it breaks. It won't break the minute your odometer hits 60,000, but don't put it off too long! Your car will have either a timing belt or a timing chain. The timing chain gets replaced only if it breaks or is very stretched. Replace the **timing belt** every 60,000 miles. Some manufacturer's recommend this at 90,000 miles—check your owner's manual. When the timing belt is replaced it is also a good time to replace the front engine seal, or crankshaft seal, and the camshaft seal. Cars with a water pump that is driven by the timing belt (instead of by a separate, external belt) should have the water pump replaced when the timing belt is changed. There is a great deal of overlap in labor time, so you will save money this way.

2. **Major tune-up** (same as 30,000-mile service).

3. **Change the differential-gear oil** (rear-wheel drive only)

4. **Change the manual-transmission oil** (to save money, this can be can be done when you get a new clutch).

5. **Replace the thermostat and the radiator cap** (should be done when the water pump is replaced).

6. **Replace the oxygen sensor** (part of the emissions system). This is often part of a 60,000-mile service. Only cars newer than around 1980 have an 02 sensor. This sensor helps the computer to adjust the air/fuel mixture. If it is not working correctly your car will get bad gas mileage. Some cars have an emissions light that will go on at 60,000 miles or 100,000 miles, reminding you to service your emissions system.

7. **Replace the belts**. Your car will have at least one belt, the alternator belt and water-pump

belt. It may also have a power-steering belt, an air-conditioner belt, an air-pump (smog) belt, and a fan belt. To save money, replace the belts when the timing belt is changed so you won't have to pay any extra labor.

Getting Ready for a Road Trip

You are about to drive from New York to California with all three of your cats in the car. It's crucial that your car be in good working order. What if you break down in the middle of a cornfield?

Make an appointment with your mechanic at least a few weeks before your road trip. Don't wait until the day before you plan to leave to make any repairs or get a tune-up.

Some garages sell a trip check. Find out exactly

what they check, then give them this list of things you expect your mechanic to check before you set out on a long trip.

Pre–Road Trip Checklist

☑ Check all the fluids

☑ Check the belts and hoses

☑ Look for any leaks

☑ Check and fill all the tires, including the spare tire

☑ Check the tire condition

☑ Four-wheel brake check

☑ Check the condition of the exhaust system

☑ Flush the cooling system (if not done in the last year)

☑ Pressure-check the cooling system (to check for leaks)

☑ Load-test the battery (to test its ability to hold a charge)

☑ Check the alternator output (to make sure the charging system is working well)

☑ Change the spark-plug wires (if more than two years old)

Other Maintenance: Parts That Commonly Wear Out or Just Plain Break

Many car owners act completely surprised when their car needs work. Besides the regular maintenance and tune-ups your car requires, parts wear out or simply break. This is normal. Even if you take extra special care of your car and follow a rigid maintenance schedule, there will be times when it will need work. There may be major repairs as your car gets older. If you are prepared for this and have realistic expectations about being a car owner, you can avoid having a nervous breakdown the next time something goes wrong.

Even if you have a brand-new car, you may be paying for repairs above and beyond general maintenance items. If something breaks on a new car it is probably still covered by the warranty. Call the dealer before you pay for repairs at an independent shop.

Owner's manuals do not include information about the replacement of parts that commonly wear out on cars—things like the brakes and the

tires and the battery and the clutch. Where and how you drive will affect how often certain things wear out. Stop and go driving in a hilly city will wear out brakes and clutches. If you live near the ocean or in a place where the roads are salted in the winter, rust can be a problem. Rust accelerates the deterioration of metal parts, like the exhaust system and the radiator. If you live on a bumpy dirt road, or use your car for transporting heavy loads, you may need the shock absorbers or struts replaced more frequently.

1. All cars need new **brakes** periodically. How often depends on your driving habits and where you live. San Franciscans can expect to get new brakes more often than people who live in Kansas. Cars with automatic transmissions need brakes more often than manual transmission cars. Trucks and heavier vehicles wear out brakes quicker than small economy cars. Don't wait until you hear noise to get the brakes checked!

2. When you get a brake job it is also a good time to have the **wheel bearings** repacked with fresh grease. Some cars have sealed wheel bearings and cannot be repacked.

3. A **battery** lasts only four or five years. Why not replace it before it leaves you stranded? You can have your battery tested to see if it still holds a good charge. This is called a battery load test. At the same time, ask your mechanic to test the alternator output to check how much current your alternator is creating. Mechanics use a special machine for both of these tests.

4. The average car needs a new **clutch** every 50,000–60,000 miles.

5. Depending on road conditions and your personal driving habits, most cars need new **tires** about every three or four years.

6. Most cars need a periodic **wheel alignment**. Some cars require a four-wheel alignment. If you drive in the city and do a lot a curbside parallel parking, it's enough to bang your car out of alignment. If you get in an accident, even a small fender bender, get an alignment.

7. Some cars have an **emissions reminder light** that comes on at a certain 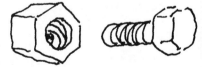 mileage, usually at 60,000 miles. This is a reminder that the oxygen sensor should be changed and other emissions equipment should be checked. Have your mechanic check the tailpipe emissions and make any air/fuel mixture adjustments at this time. The light does not mean that anything is broken, it is a maintenance *reminder* light. It shouldn't cost much to have the light turned off, but you will have to pay for a proper emissions system check.

8. You can expect that during the lifetime of your car (or before 120,000 miles) you will probably need a new **alternator, starter,** and **water pump**. If your car has a water pump that is driven by the timing belt, it's a good idea to get the water pump replaced when the timing belt is replaced, even if it's not broken. You'll save money on labor by doing it this way. When the water pump goes, make sure the **thermostat** and **radiator cap** get replaced too. The thermostat is an inexpensive part that can cause your engine to overheat if it fails.

9. Your car will need a new set of **shocks** or **struts** at least once or twice during its life, depending on your driving habits. Struts are more expensive to replace than shocks, although they do the same job of giving you a smooth ride. Some cars have struts *and* shocks (one type in the front and another in the back).

10. The **exhaust system**, underneath the car (muffler and exhaust pipes), will probably need replacing before your car reaches 60,000 miles. If there is snow and ice where you live, and the roads are salted, you can expect to pay for exhaust-system repairs frequently. The salt and weather cause the metal to rust and corrode.

11. Many cars that survive past 150,000 miles will need a rebuilt or new **transmission** (automatic or manual). You can avoid costly repairs by getting a **transmission service** (change the ATF and filter or gear oil) every two years or 24,000 miles. Take care of any leaks before low gear oil causes damage to your transmission.

12. It is not unusual for older cars (over 100,000 miles) to need a new **fuel pump**.

13. Little stuff like **headlights, bulbs** for taillights and turn signals, **windshield-wiper blades**, and **fuses** will need to be replaced as they wear or burn out.

How Much Does It Cost to Own a Car?

Owning a car is privilege many of us take for granted. We often have unrealistic expectations about what it takes to care for our cars and what it costs to be a car owner. The more unrealistic and uninformed our expectations, the lower our serenity level.

For those who enjoy number crunching and keeping lists, there is a fairly simply method to find out exactly how much you are spending, per mile, to own your car. Add up the total yearly costs of the following expenses, and divide by the number of miles you drive in a year. This will work even if you choose to approximate.

- **Buying a car**: down payment, sales tax, cost of repairs when you buy a used car.
- **Ownership costs**: registration, monthly payments, interest, and license fees.
- **Maintenance costs**: gasoline and oil changes, tires and brakes, tune-ups, and regular service.
- **Repairs and towing**: unexpected repairs, including accidents and body work.
- **Parking costs**: parking-garage fees and parking tickets.
- **Depreciation**: the value of your car when you buy it minus the value of your car when you sell it.
- **Bad-driving fees**: moving violations, traffic school.
- **Damage to the environment**: It's hard to put a real dollar sign on this one. I love to drive as much as the next guy, but you gotta admit, the planet is paying a pretty hefty price.

Chapter 8

What Is a Tune-Up?

There's a lot of confusion about what a tune-up is. Simply put, a tune-up is when certain worn parts are replaced and specific adjustments are made to your car to make it run smoothly. Even a so-called self-tuning engine needs to have at least the air and fuel filters replaced and the spark plugs changed. Some people don't call this a tune-up, but it still needs to be done or even-

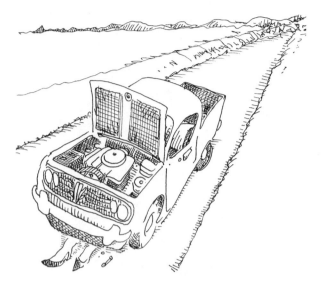

tually your car won't run well, or at all. Your car needs regular tune-ups (usually every 30,000 miles) in addition to the suggested maintenance listed in the previous chapter.

Your owner's manuals may not refer to anything called a tune-up, and garages offer different variations of what is included in a complete tune-up. If you have a late model (newer) car, some parts of a tune-up are not applicable to your particular car. You may be paying for something you don't need. A tune-up on a 1976 car and a 1996 car will look very different.

When a customer calls and asks for a tune-up, I always ask her why she thinks she needs one. The correct answer is, "I've just reached x number of miles and it's been 30,000 miles since the car was last tuned-up." If your car is overheating or making a new noise or stalling, for example, there's a good chance a tune-up will not fix the problem. A tune-up is not a cure all for every car problem. But if you put off the recommended maintenance on your car long enough, eventually you will have drivability problems. Cars often come in for repairs that cannot be diagnosed until a tune-up has first been done to rule out likely problem components (spark plugs, filters, spark plug wires, etc.). In this scenario you'll end up paying for a tune-up as well as for the diagnosis and repair of any other problems.

Your car should get a tune-up (or major service) every two years (or 30,000 miles). Here is a list of what a tune-up should include. Some things may not apply to your particular car. Check your owner's manual and read the following, which explains this list in detail.

1. Replace the **air filter**. All cars need to have the air filter changed as part of a tune-up.

2. Replace the **fuel filter**. Some cars have two fuel filters, and often only one gets changed. If you drive on dusty roads you will have to change the air and fuel filters more frequently. Some shops sell fuel-injection cleaning as regular maintenance. Unless the fuel injectors are clogged, this is not necessary. Premium gasoline has special detergents and cleaning agents in it that do the job of keeping the fuel injectors clean. Changing the fuel filter every 30,000

miles is the best maintenance for your fuel system.

3. Replacing the **spark plugs** is always part of a tune-up. Many new cars with platinum spark plugs need the plugs changed only every 60,000 miles.

4. A new set of high-quality spark-plug wires will make your bill a little higher, but is well worth the cost. Some cars have spark-plug wires that are permanently attached to the distributor cap, so they both have to be changed at the same time.

5. Most cars need a new **distributor cap** and **rotor** as part of a tune-up. Some newer cars have distributorless ignition and therefore won't need this.

6. Cars with adjustable valves need a **valve adjustment**. Not just old cars need valve adjustments, either. But if your car has hydraulic valves the valves cannot be adjusted. When you get a valve adjustment be sure the valve-cover gasket is replaced. It is very common for valve-cover gaskets to leak, so if you see oil around the top of the engine, be sure this gets checked.

7. Older cars without electronic ignition (about 1978 and earlier) need to have the **points** and **condenser** changed. Setting the dwell and the timing should be included when the points are

changed. If your car has points, you may want to change, or at least adjust, them more often (every six months) than you do the other parts of a tune-up. When the points are changed make sure the ignition timing is checked at the same time.

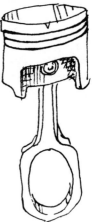

8. Check the **ignition timing**. On cars with electronic ignition the timing usually doesn't change, but it's a good idea to check it as part of a tune-up. On some cars the timing is not adjustable.

9. If your car is **fuel-injected** (does not have a carburetor) part of a tune-up includes cleaning the throttle plate. On some fuel-injected cars the air/fuel mixture can be adjusted during a tune-up, on others it cannot. If your car has a **carburetor** it may need an adjustment. (All cars either have a carburetor or are fuel injected.) There are two adjustments possible: idle speed adjustment and air/fuel mixture adjustment. On most newer cars it is not possible to adjust the air/fuel mixture during a tune-up.

10. **Checking the fluids** under the hood may be part of what you are paying for in a tune-up. This is something you should already be doing yourself on a regular basis. Some shops do not include this in a tune-up, although they should.

11. Adjusting the **clutch** can be part of a tune-up. Some cars with manual transmissions have self-adjusting clutches.

12. Servicing the **battery** should be part of a major tune-up. This includes cleaning the battery terminals and cable ends, and in some batteries, adding distilled water. Corroded battery terminals can keep your car from starting.

13. The **PCV** (positive crankcase ventilation) **valve** should also be replaced during a tune-up. This is a very inexpensive part and not difficult to change. A clogged PCV valve can cause your car to run rough or stall.

Chapter 9

Car Talk:

How to Sound Like You Know What You're Talking About

Talking to Mechanics

Miscommunication between customers and mechanics arises for a number of reasons. If the consumer (you) doesn't know the first thing about cars, communication is difficult. If you are willing to listen and learn, you are already halfway there. Unfortunately, not all mechanics want to take the time to explain to you what's wrong with your car. As far as I'm concerned, this is part of the job of being a mechanic. If you visit the doctor and he or she won't take the time to explain what's going on with your body, you'd probably start looking for another doctor. You should do the same if a mechanic won't explain what your car needs and why.

Another factor to take into account is that while many mechanics are very mechanically and technically skilled, they may be a little deficient in what we call people skills. Think about it; they're not even nerds. But with a little prompting and interest, even the shyest gearhead loves to talk about cars. Just remember that there's no such thing as a stupid question. Don't hesitate to ask the same question again if you don't understand the answer. If you feel like you're being talked down to, take your business elsewhere. You are not stupid just because you don't understand everything about your car. You're not the mechanic, you shouldn't be expected to know it all before you drive through the door.

Try to talk with the mechanic who will be working on your car when you bring it in for service. Important information can get lost in the translation between the service manager (person behind the desk) and the person who will be fixing your car. Ask the mechanic who will be working on your car to go on a test drive with you if your car needs diagnosing for a drivability problem or a noise.

Resist the urge to ask for a diagnosis over the phone. Customers often call and explain the symptoms and expect to immediately find out what the problem is and how much it will cost to fix. If auto repair were that easy it would be way cheaper.

Bring the following information with you when you go to the garage:

- Year, make, and model of your car
- Copies of previous repair orders
- Knowledge of exactly what you are bringing the car in for. You should have a clear idea of what the symptoms are and how long they have been occurring.

Identifying and Describing Symptoms

Before you bring your car in for a repair, gather up all the information you can that may be helpful in explaining what's going on. If it's a noise, pay attention to it when you hear it: Is it only on the highway, only when you go over a bump, when turning left, in third gear? If it's a drivability problem, do the same: do you only experience the symptom first thing in the morning,

going up hills, over 45 miles per hour? Exactly how long has that dashboard light been on? It can be frustrating to bring your car in to get it fixed and then it acts just fine when you get to the shop. This might be because the problem is evident only under certain conditions. If you know what these conditions are, it may cost you less in the amount of time it takes to find the problem.

The Fifth Law of Auto Repair states that there is a 60 percent chance you car will be just fine by the time you arrive at the shop. (Kind of like having a good hair day just when you've scheduled an appointment for a haircut.) An intermittent problem is as frustrating to the mechanic trying to fix the car as it is for you. You might have to leave your car at the shop for repeated test drives in hopes that it will eventually act up or bring it back when the symptom gets worse. Pay closer attention to when the car exhibits the symptoms. If the car stalls first thing in the morning, but is fine once it warms up, you might have to leave it overnight, for example.

Symptom Checklist

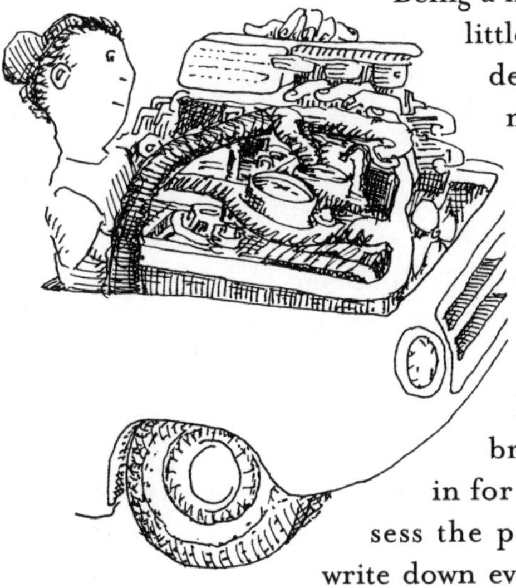

Being a mechanic is a little like being a detective. The more clues your mechanic has the easier it is to diagnose a problem. Before you bring your car in for a repair, assess the problem and write down everything you can think of that might help your mechanic find out what's wrong. Every clue helps! Use the following symptom checklist to help describe what's wrong with you car.

- **What's the problem?**
  Sound
  Smell
  Leak
  Vibration or shimmy
  Drivability/performance problem

Handling, steering, or suspension
Brakes
Dashboard lights

· **When does it happen?**
When the car is cold
Fully warmed up
In the morning, only when it's raining, etc.

· **Under what driving conditions?**
All the time
Only on the highway
When the brake or clutch pedal is depressed
Under 20 mph
When turning left or right
In third gear (in reverse, neutral, etc.)
Up hills, etc.

· **How long has it been happening?**
Since yesterday, the last six months, forever.

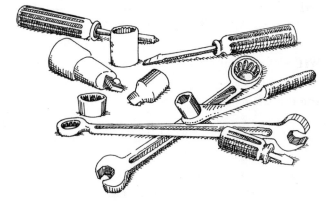

Necessary Vocabulary

If you have a little vocabulary under your belt, talking to mechanics will be easier because you'll both be speaking the same language. People call and say, "Ren, my car isn't working," or, "My car won't start." You can't get any vaguer than that. (Except one of my favorites: "Help, my car is dead!"). We usually spend the next twenty minutes over the phone trying to translate—time that could be spent fixing the car!

To begin with, don't use the term "turn over" when talking about your car. It's confusing because some people mean "crank" when they say "turn over" and some people mean "start." Cranking is the term used to describe the starter motor turning the engine. This happens only when you have the key turned all the way to the right, in the spring-loaded position. It sounds like this: *rrr-rrr-rrr-rrr-rrr.*

Use the Following Terms When Talking to Mechanics

- **Will not crank**: When you turn the key, nothing happens. Silence. Or maybe a clicking noise.

- **Cranks slowly but will not start**: The engine cranks (*rrr-rrr-rrr*), but slower than usual. If you keep trying to start it you will end up with a car that won't crank.

- **Cranks but won't start**: Cranks at normal speed but will not start and stay running.
- **Starts and runs but stalls**: Starts but won't stay running.
- **Starts and runs but will not go**: Engine idles fine but when you put it in gear and give it gas, nothing happens; the car doesn't move forward.

Common Car Sounds and Words That Describe Them

bang	like a firecracker
buzzing	like a very loud bee
clicking	like the sound of a light switch being turned off and on
clunk	the neighbors upstairs just dropped an iron skillet
creak	like a rusty door hinge or old floor boards
grinding	metal against metal, or ice skates on concrete
knocking	like rapping on a table with your knuckles
hissing	like an old steam radiator or letting air out of a balloon
pinging	shaking a jar of popcorn
rattle	like a baby's rattle
rubbing	like dragging a burlap sack full of potatoes across the room
rumbling	like thunder far away
squeak	like a mouse or a squeak toy

squeal	like a long and very high pitched whistle, loud bird whistling
tapping	like castanets or tap shoes
whirring	like a fan with a piece of paper caught in it

Common Car Problems and What They Sound or Feel Like

backfire: A very loud bang, like a gunshot. Can come from the back of the car or from the engine.

brake pulsation: When you put your foot on the brake there is a vibration at the pedal.

bucking: The engine stumbles causing the entire car to lurch.

cutting out: The car loses power for an instant.

grabby brakes: The car stops short even when you step lightly on the brake pedal.

dieseling: The engine still runs after you turn the key off.

exhaust leak: Sounds like a Harley motorcycle. An exhaust leak can be anywhere from the engine to the muffler.

hesitation: A delayed reaction between the gas pedal and the car's speed.

missing (or **misfire**): When the engine is not running on all its cylinders; you will notice lack of power and the engine will feel like it's running rough.

play in the steering: The steering feels loose; there is a delay between turning the steering wheel and the wheels' turning.

pulling: When you are driving down a straight, flat road the car drifts in one direction; can also happen when braking.

rough idle or **uneven idle**: When you are in Park or Neutral the engine runs rough and the car shakes or feels like it might stall.

slipping clutch or transmission: The engine revs when you give it gas; the amount of gas you are giving the engine does not correspond to how fast you are going. On a manual transmission, you will have to downshift more frequently to get the amount of power you are used to, which is most noticeable on hills.

sluggish: Low on power, can't get up hills very well, poor acceleration.

spongy brakes: The brake pedal feels soft. It may also pump up (get harder if you pump the brakes).

stalls: Car stops running at stoplights or won't stay running if you take your foot off the gas pedal.

surge: Feels as if you are giving it gas even if you're not.

revving high: In Park or Neutral the engine sounds like you have your foot on the gas even if you don't.

vacuum leak: Air is being sucked in where it shouldn't be, making the gas mixture lean (diluted). Engine idles rough and feels like it might stall.

vibration: A shaking you can feel inside the car.

Smells

Oil: An oil leak that is dripping onto any hot part of the exhaust will smell nasty as it burns off. Open the hood and look for signs of oil leaking. Check the oil and see if it's low. Fix oil leaks as they happen.

Exhaust: Exhaust is gas after it has burned. This smell could indicate a leak in the exhaust system; the exhaust is coming into the car instead of being diverted out the tailpipe. You can also hear an exhaust leak, and it will get louder as the leak gets bigger. A hole in the exhaust system sounds a little like a motorcycle with a noisy muffler. Carbon monoxide can make you dizzy and give you headaches, and in large enough doses it is fatal. Take care of this right away! Sometimes worn weather stripping on a hatchback can cause an exhaust smell inside the car, even if there is no exhaust leak.

Gas: The smell of raw, unburned gasoline means there may be a leak somewhere. First check that you haven't left the gas cap off. A gas leak should be taken care of right away, because it could potentially cause a fire.

Rotten-egg smell: Can indicate a very rich mixture (too much gas, not enough air) or possibly a plugged up catalytic converter.

Rubber: The smell of burning rubber can mean that a rubber hose is touching something hot and melting, or a that pulley that drives a belt is locked up and the belt is about to disintegrate.

Plastic: Check underneath the car to see if a

plastic bag is melted to the exhaust. It stinks like crazy when this happens. A smell of burning plastic can also be caused by the insulation around electrical wires burning, indicating a short that could be causing a fire. If you see smoke coming from under the hood, turn off the ignition. Release the hood latch from inside the car but don't open the hood. Then call the fire department.

Brake and clutch: The material on the brake pads and shoes and the lining of the clutch disc are made from the same stuff. If the clutch is slipping (needs to be replaced soon because there is no more "clutching" material left) or the brakes are getting too hot, you may smell a peculiar and unpleasant chemical scent, like when you drive through certain parts of New Jersey. It's hard to describe, but you usually smell it after driving on hills or in heavy stop-and-go traffic.

And just a little reminder:

Left side of the car is always the driver's side.

Right side of the car is always the passenger side. (To avoid confusion, this is recognized by mechanics and parts people anywhere in the country.)

Chapter 10

Bringing Your Car to the Shop

Finding a Mechanic You Can Trust

For many people the hardest part of owning a car is dealing with mechanics. If you own a car, at

121

one time or another you will have to bring it to a repair shop. This is true even if your car is new and doesn't need repairs. You will still need to bring it to the shop for maintenance. Many car owners experience being talked down to, ignored, or made to feel stupid when they get their car worked on. This is completely unnecessary. If a service writer (person behind the desk at a garage) or a mechanic treats you with condescension it's time to find another shop. And tell them why you are taking your business elsewhere.

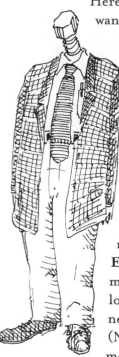

Here are some things you will want to factor in when deciding where to bring your car for service or repair.

Recommendations:
Referrals by friends and coworkers is always the best place to start. A customer of mine found me by putting signs on all the Hondas on her block asking for a good Honda mechanic!
Expertise: Do they work on many cars like yours? How long have they been in business? Are the mechanics ASE (National Institute for Automotive Service Excellence) certified?

Personal interactions: Do the employees treat you with respect? Do they explain things to you?

Price: You should definitely shop around for a good price, but just because a shop charges a lot doesn't guarantee quality. Inversely, the very inexpensive chain stores have a reputation for shoddy work.

Warranty: Most reputable shops will guarantee their work for at least three months, and some warranty for six or twelve months. Ask about the warranty before they work on your car and find out if it covers parts *and* labor.

Time: Will the job be done in a timely fashion or will your car sit in the shop and gather dust until they get around to fixing it? What are the shop's hours? Will you have to take time off work to drop your car off and pick it up?

Location: Is the garage near your home or work? Near a bus or a train line? If not, do they offer rides or a shuttle to customers? Do they offer a loaner car?

Licenses and affiliations: All automotive repair shops should have a business license, like any other business. The garage may also be accredited by the Better Business Bureau and AAA (Automobile Association of America). Also look for mechanics that are ASE certified.

Finding a shop or mechanic you feel you can trust can be as difficult as finding a good lover. Don't wait until your car needs major work to find a repair shop you want to do business with. If your car is broken and needs to be towed, you won't have the time to shop around, and you may end up at a garage out of desperation, not choice. Make a point of using a shop a few times for maintenance and little stuff to see if you like the service before bringing your car in for major repairs.

Finally, don't bring your car in for major repairs right before you go on a long trip. If the car needs major work or a part needs to be ordered, you may have to change your plans. If a part turns out to be defective (it happens) or the job was done wrong, you are better off being at home so you can bring the car back to the shop (under warranty) rather than being stuck in the middle of nowhere paying to get the job done again.

Getting Your Car Fixed Right—the First Time

Never go into a shop and ask them to "do whatever it needs." Use your owner's manual and the maintenance schedule beginning on page 86 to keep track of when to bring your car in for service. Find out exactly what repairs are going to be done and how much it will cost before the work begins. The shop must give you a written estimate when you bring your car in. A shop may not do any work on your car without prior authorization. This is the law.

You may have to leave your car for diagnosing and then give verbal authorization for repairs over the phone. This should be noted on your work order. Diagnosing (finding out what the problem is) will often cost money in itself, separate from the cost of the actual repairs and parts. You will authorize a certain amount of time just for diagnosing, and then give the OK for the parts and labor once the mechanic has found out what's wrong. Even if you decide to bring your car elsewhere for the repairs, you still must pay for the time spent diagnosing.

Do not go into a garage and tell them to "replace x," even if you are fairly certain you know what the problem is. Ask them to diagnose the noise or symptom and then give you an estimate, even if the car was already diagnosed elsewhere. You may think it's your starter, for example, and ask them to replace it, but if that's not the problem you will still have to pay for a starter you didn't need—they were only following your directions. A good mechanic should always diagnose the problem before replacing parts, but unfortunately this doesn't always happen. This is a gray area that can end up costing you money if you're not careful.

Don't hesitate to get a second opinion if something doesn't sound right. If you are quoted a price that seems very high, make a few phone calls, and find out what is the going rate for that particular job. If the car isn't running, there's no reason why you can't get it towed a second time if you decide you don't want to do business with the first shop you picked.

REPAIR ORDER

LABOR	
LUBRICATION	O
CHANGE OIL	O
FILTER CART.	O
CHANGE TRANS.	O
CHANGE DIFF.	O
ADJUST BRAKES	O
ROTATE TIRES	O
WASH POLISH	O
STATE INSPECTION	O

TOTAL LABOR	
TOTAL PARTS	
ACCESSORIES	
GAS, OIL, & GREASE	
OUTSIDE REPAIRS	
TAX	
TOTAL AMOUNT	

NAME		DATE
ADDRESS		
MAKE	TYPE OR MODEL	YEAR
SERIAL NO.	ENGINE NO.	
SPEEDOMETER	LICENSE NO.	
ORDER WRITTEN BY		PHONE

SPECIAL INSTRUCTIONS

You are entitled to a price estimate for the repairs you have authorized.
The repair price may be less than the estimate, but will not exceed the
estimate without your permission.

Estimate: _____

MATERIAL USED

QUAN.	PART NO.	DESCRIPTION	PRICE
		TOTAL PARTS	
		TOTAL ACCESSORIES	

A TYPICAL AUTO REPAIR ORDER/RECEIPT.

Types of Repair Shops

Dealership: Dealerships sell and repair new and used cars and focus on one or two brands of cars. The advantage of bringing your car to the dealership is that the mechanics are usually specialists in your particular car. They have up-to-date diagnostic equipment and are knowledgeable about performance problems specific to your car. The disadvantage is that they charge more than most other shops, and you will probably never get to talk with the person who actually works on your car. It can be a very impersonal encounter. For most maintenance items you can get a better deal elsewhere. If your car is still under warranty and you bring it somewhere other than the dealer, find out if they are using original factory parts. Some warranties are voided if aftermarket parts are used.

Specialty shop: This is a shop that fixes only certain types of cars or works only on certain systems. For instance, you might choose to go to a shop that works only on German cars if you drive a BMW. The mechanics will know more about your particular car and its quirks. A specialty shop could also be a garage that does only transmission repair or specializes in electrical problems (not to be confused with discount auto repair chains).

Independent repair shop: This is probably the kind of shop you are most familiar with. Family-run garages and gas stations, high-tech diagnostic and repair shops, and everything in between fall into this category. Quality at privately owned, independent shops runs the gamut. Independent shops are good for tune-ups, brakes, maintenance, and most general repairs. Smaller shops sometimes subcontract particular types of repair jobs to other garages—they are acting as the middleman and charging you for it. Find out if all the work being done on your car is at the garage or if they are sending it out to another shop.

Discount chains: There are many large nation-wide discount auto repair chains, usually franchised. They often run ads in local papers offering unbelievably cheap prices. Sometimes they even offer "free" services, like a free brake check. Nothing is free, so when you drive in for a free service you will probably end up being sold something, whether you need it or not. In addition, the prices advertised are not always what you will end up paying by the time the job is done, and you'll often be given the hard sell on everything else your car needs "right away." These shops have a high employee turnover and don't pay their mechanics very well; the pros are probably not working there. It's OK to get your oil changed at a chain, but don't let them sell you an air filter every time you drive through! Discount chains and department-store chains can be a bargain for simple stuff like batteries, tires, mufflers, and window replacement.

Street mechanic: This may be your next-door neighbor who knows very little about auto repair or a professional mechanic who does side work on the weekends. You're taking your chances unless you know and trust this mechanic, because you will have no legal recourse if something isn't fixed correctly. Some professional and honest mechanics will do side work at a much lower price than you would find anywhere else (they have no overhead), but be wary if it's someone you don't know well.

Parts

Find out what kind of parts are being used in your car. Quality and expense can vary greatly when it comes to parts.

OEM (original equipment manufacturer): Original factory parts can be purchased only from the dealer and almost always cost more than aftermarket parts. Things like body trim, interior parts and accessories are always dealer items.

Aftermarket: Any part that is not made by the manufacturer of your particular car is considered an aftermarket part. You can ask what brand will be used in your car, but without doing a little research this is useless information. You can

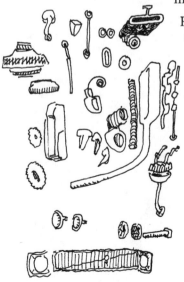

PUT IT ALL TOGETHER AND WHAT DO YOU GET?

A VACUUM CLEANER?

call parts stores and ask which are quality brands for your car.

Rebuilt or remanufactured: Not brand new, but the essential or defective components of the part are replaced or reconditioned. In many cases using a rebuilt part is standard practice, because the factory part is extremely expensive. Examples of commonly used rebuilt parts are starters, alternators, axles, and transmissions. The same warranty should apply for rebuilt parts as for new ones.

Used: Used parts are either bought from a junkyard or taken from a retired car. There is usually no warranty on used parts. If the part is defective or fails soon after, you will have to pay for labor again and another replacement part. You are always taking a chance with used parts.

Settling for the cheapest parts is not always the wisest thing to do. If the part fails two months later while you are on a trip, you haven't saved any money. Most shops will not guarantee a part if you purchased it yourself, either.

Many customers are resentful when they learn that a part was marked up. All garages mark up the cost of parts. This covers potential replacement of failed parts under warranty and the time and energy spent researching and obtaining the correct part.

While Your Car Is at the Shop

Figure out alternative methods of transportation before you need to bring your car to the shop.

What buses run near your house? Can you catch a ride to work with a coworker? Is there air in your bicycle tires? If you know how to get around without a car, you'll be less freaked out while yours is being fixed.

Be sure to be available by phone when you leave your car, or call in every couple of hours. If you drop your car off for an oil change and a brake check and you need brakes, you'll have to authorize the brake work over the phone. If the shop can't reach you, the car will sit all day without getting fixed.

Give the garage enough time to work on your car. Just because you get a quote of two hours doesn't mean you can drop your car off at 2:00 P.M. and get it back exactly at 4:00. Parts have to be ordered and picked up, the work order needs to be written up, and the job may take longer than two hours even if you only get charged for two.

Standing over the mechanic and tapping your foot won't make it go any faster. Besides, why would you want to rush the person fixing your car—that's when mistakes are made. Some mechanics don't mind if you watch, but be sure to ask first. Having someone stand over your shoulder while you work can be nerve-racking, no matter what line of work you're in. This doesn't mean that you can't be shown what is being replaced or repaired. In many cases your mechanic should be able to point out what is going on. For instance, if a mechanic says your car has an oil leak, ask to see it. You can see a leak with your own eyes. If a new CV boot is recommended because the old one is torn, ask to see the ripped boot before you give the OK. Obviously, there are some things you can't see, but it doesn't hurt to ask and you'll learn a little in the process.

While working on your car, your mechanic may find other things wrong. This does not mean that the shop is trying to rip you off or sell you unnecessary repairs. It may mean you have an observant mechanic. If you feel like you're getting a hard sell, or have any reason to doubt the suggested repairs, you should always go somewhere else for a second opinion.

Always call and ask if your car is ready before coming by to pick it up. Any mechanic will tell you that the second Law of Auto Repair States: "If the customer comes to get her car without calling first there's a 90 percent chance it won't be ready." This is a fact.

What to Do If Your Car Isn't Fixed Right

Always go for a test-drive before you pay the bill. If something wasn't fixed right you can deal with it immediately without the hassle of having paid and driven home.

If you brought your car in for a repair and it still has the same problem a day later—go back! Assume they will right the problem until you know for sure that you are being blown off. Make sure you bring all the paperwork. Most shops will warranty their work, but the longer you wait the harder it may be to get them to honor the warranty. A "comeback" (failed part or a job not done right, in shop lingo) is every mechanic's worst nightmare. Comebacks should be top priority. They should let you know that your car will be one of the first looked at. If the job was done incorrectly or a part failed, it should be fixed at no extra charge to you.

It's a good idea to pay with a credit card because if you end up having a dispute over prices or repairs you can deal with it through the credit card company. If you've paid cash or written a check that's already cleared and think you are owed money back it may be very difficult to get reimbursed.

Sometimes something different will go wrong with your car after you've had it in the shop. It may be related to the work that was done, but it could also be coincidental. First, don't jump to conclusions. Bring the car back and see what they find. If you believe the problem relates to the work done, but the shop disagrees, call around for another opinion. If you need a new starter two days after you had brakes, it's just bad luck, the two systems are completely unrelated. But if your car starts overheating after you've had the belts replaced, it *might* be related (maybe the water pump belt is loose, for example). Not all situations are as obvious as these examples, which is why you might need more than one professional opinion.

If you think you've been had and the shop is being completely uncooperative, you can call either the Better Business Bureau or the agency in your state that regulates the automotive repair industry. Your state attorney general's office is the best place to start if you can't personally work things out. In many cases they will send out a mediator. If you have another mechanic that you trust, he or she might also be willing to get on the phone and try to hammer it out as well.

Ways to Avoid Getting Ripped Off

It would be a near perfect world if all mechanics were honest, but the truth is the automotive field, like any other business, has its share of shysters. Short of becoming a mechanic, or marrying one, being knowledgeable and prepared is your best defense.

1. Take the time to find a garage you feel good about. Bring your car in for maintenance or minor repairs before trusting a shop with major work.

2. Don't bring your car in right before going on a trip out of town. If something isn't fixed right you'll be too far away from the garage that did the work to deal with it.

3. When in doubt, get a second opinion. Call other shops for estimates before giving authorization for repairs. If your car is disabled and you don't trust the diagnosis or estimate, there's no reason why you can't tow it to another shop.

4. Always ask for a written estimate before the job is started. Write "No repairs authorized without owner's consent" on the work order.

5. Find out what the shop's warranty policy is beforehand.

6. Never say, "Do whatever you think it needs." If you are bringing your car in for a 60,000-mile service, for example, read the owner's manual and make a list of exactly what needs to be done. Leave this list with your mechanic.

7. Talk to the mechanic who will be working on your car. If necessary, go on a test-drive with the person who will be fixing your car.

8. Describe the symptoms. Be clear about exactly why you are bringing the car in. Ask, "Will this repair fix this symptom?"

9. Ask for explanations. If something is leaking, torn, or needs replacing, ask to be shown.

10. Ask for your old parts back (*before* the mechanic starts the work!).

11. Be available by phone, and call in to check up on the progress of your car while it is at the shop.

12. Before paying, read the work order carefully. Ask for an explanation of anything on the work order that doesn't make sense. Make sure you get a copy of the work order—this is your receipt.

13. Go for a test-drive before paying. If something isn't right, make it clear that you will leave the car and not pay until it is fixed correctly.

14. Pay with a credit card. Many credit cards offer consumer protection for fraud.

15. If you discover something is not fixed right after you've payed and driven home, go back to the shop as soon as possible.

Chapter 11

Help!

Breaking Down on the Road and Other Scary Stuff

Can I Panic Now?

You're cruising down a lonely country road, the wind in your hair and your favorite tunes on the radio. Suddenly—your worst nightmare—your car starts acting funny. What do you do?

First, don't panic. It only makes everything harder to deal with. There are a number of situations you will be able to take care of, as you will learn in this chapter. The first thing to remember is to keep yourself safe as you pull off the road. Put the right blinker on as you make your way over to the right shoulder, and when you are off the road put on the hazard lights. Be careful of soft shoulders and don't pull off the road on a bridge, overpass, or underpass unless you have no choice. Try not to park near a bend in the road; that makes you less visible to oncoming traffic. Take care when getting out of the car. Get out from the passenger side, especially if you are on a highway.

Put the hood up, even if the problem is a flat tire. This indicates that you are pulled over because you have car problems. Otherwise, people might think you're just taking a pee. If you have reflector triangles put them on the ground at least fifteen feet behind your car. It's a good idea to have reflector triangles in the trunk of your car. They are easier to use than flares, and they won't fall apart after sitting in the trunk for years. A white cloth or piece of clothing hanging from the antennae or rear view mirror is also a universal distress signal.

If you are a woman alone and you feel uncomfortable about walking to the next exit/garage/phone, then stay in your car. It may be a long time until someone stops, though. If you have a "call police" or "help" sign, put it in the back window. Stay in the car with the doors locked. When someone stops, open the window a crack. Ask them to call a tow truck or the police rather than take a ride from a stranger.

I think you should always do a little investigation when something goes wrong on the road. Determine what type of problem you have: drivability/performance (engine), handling (tires, steering, or suspension), brakes, etc. Is it a light, a sound, a smell, or a leak? Where is it coming from: under the hood, inside the car, back or front of the car, etc. Check it out! Look around a little. Open the hood and see if any wires or hoses are disconnected or broken. Set aside the voice in your head that's telling you, "I'm screwed, my car just broke down in the middle of nowhere." With that voice comes panic, which makes us overlook the obvious. I've had more than a few cars towed to the shop that had nothing wrong with them other than an empty gas tank. Check the gas gauge, look at the fuses, do an all-around sniff test. This chapter will guide you through what sort of things you can look for when something's not right. And if it turns out to be something more serious than you can handle on the side of the road, don't stress, just read Chapter 10 on finding a good mechanic.

The Emergency Tool Kit

Here is a list of items you should have in the trunk of your car.

All the necessary equipment to change a tire (working jack, spare tire, lugnut wrench, pipe for leverage)

Flashlight with fresh batteries

Triangle reflectors or flares

Rags and a funnel

Two quarts of oil (10W-40)

Gallon of water and antifreeze

Brake fluid

Power-steering fluid (if applicable)

Automatic-transmission fluid (if applicable)

Jumper cables (at least 8 feet long)

Work gloves or latex gloves

Blanket

AAA or roadside emergency card

Spare fuses

Optional: A good book, a bathing suit, snacks

What to Check If . . .

Here's a list of items anyone, no matter how mechanically challenged, can check out when things go wrong. Some of this stuff may seem ridiculously obvious, but when something's wrong with your car it's easy to overlook the obvious.

Brakes

What you can check:
· Brake-fluid level (see page 45)
· Hand brake on?

Car won't start (does not crank—no sound)

What you can check:
· Transmission in Park, foot on brake?
· Clutch pedal depressed?

- Seat belt on? (Some cars won't start unless the seat belt is on!)
- See Chapter 6 on jump-starting and batteries.
- Follow the positive-battery cable to the starter motor. Check for loose connections at the starter.

Car won't start (cranks but doesn't start)

What you can check:
- Out of gas?
- Look under the hood for disconnected hoses or wires.
- The fuses—especially fuses labeled "fuel pump" or "fuel injection." See page 27 on how to tell if a fuse is blown and how to change a fuse.

Clutch problems

What you can check:
- Clutch fluid (see page 49)
- Look behind the pedal to see if the clutch cable is broken or disconnected. Open the hood and find where the clutch cable comes through from the pedal. Follow the cable to the transmission to see if it's connected.

Dead battery (won't crank or cranks slowly)

See Chapter 6 on jump-starting.

Key broken in ignition switch

Use profanities. Call a locksmith or a mechanic.

Keys are lost

I won't tell you that you should always have a spare set of keys, because you already know that, right? Here's the deal: All car keys have a four-digit key code stamped on them. With this number you can have the dealer make you a new key. Obviously, since you lost the only set of keys, you probably don't have this number, either. But you can also find the key code on the trunk lock or door cylinders. It's written very small, and usually the locks will have to be removed first in order to see it. A locksmith can also help you make a new key, although this will be expensive.

Flat tire

See Chapter 5.

Lights and turn signals

What you can check:
· The fuses. See page 27 on how to tell if a fuse is blown and how to change a fuse.
· For a burned-out bulb.
· For corrosion (white gak) in the bulb socket.

Locked out

- Call a friend who has access to a spare car key.
- Many service stations have a tool for unlocking cars. Are you near any gas stations or repair shops?
- Call AAA or emergency road service.

Out of gas

- Walk to a gas station to buy some gas. You will need a gas can, and may have to purchase one in order to carry gas back. Never leave gas in a container inside your car, even in the trunk, because it is highly flammable.
- Call AAA or emergency road service; they will bring you a gallon.

Overheating or running hot

What you can check:
· The coolant level (see page 43).
· For leaks: green fluid on the ground, near hoses and radiator. Add coolant and have any leaks repaired right away.
· With the car running: Is the fan turning? If the fan is driven by a belt: Is the belt loose? If the fan is not driven by a belt, it should cycle on and off. If it doesn't, check the fuses.

Smells

What you can check:
· Where is it coming from?
· See checklist on smells on page 119.

Stalling

What you can check:
· Look under the hood for disconnected hoses or wires.

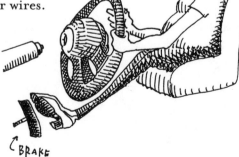

Steering trouble

What you can check:
- The power-steering fluid. If low, look for leaks.
- The belt that drives the power-steering pump.
- The tire pressure.

Transmission troubles

What you can check:
- Is the gear shifter in the car between positions?
- The automatic-transmission fluid.

Weird problems: ants and mice

I have had two different customers call me, in all seriousness, asking me if I could help them with a problem of ants and mice in their car. The obvious answer is don't be such a slob, but I didn't tell them that. For ants, that's easy, get ant traps. For the squeamish customer with the mouse problem, a trap was unacceptable. Leaving her cat in the car for a while was also not an option. I told her to leave the car doors open over night and make a trail of cheese that led into a meadow. When the moon is full, of course. I learned that in trade school.

Breakdown Reminders

1. Don't panic! Breathe deeply.

2. Put your right blinker on and get to the side of the road safely.

3. Don't pull over on a bridge, overpass, or underpass or near a sharp turn in the road.

4. Put the four-way flashers on and get out of the car on the passenger side, away from traffic. Never stand in between two cars that are on the side of the road.

5. Put the hood up to indicate your car is disabled. Put out triangle road reflectors or a "call police" sign on the back windshield. A white handkerchief or piece of cloth on the antennae is also a universal sign for surrender or help.

6. Take a moment to look under the hood or investigate where the problem might be coming from. It may be something obvious that has simply come loose, like a rubber vacuum line or a spark-plug wire. You may be out of gas, so check the gas gauge. Check the fuses to see if any are blown. Read

Chapter 2 on dashboard lights; Chapter 4 on checking fluids; and Chapter 5 on how to change a tire.

7. Stay in the car with the windows up and the door locked after you've determined that you really can't drive to safety. Wear your seat belts whenever waiting in a disabled car. Don't take a ride from anyone who seems creepy, ask them to call the highway patrol or a tow truck. If you know there is a roadside call box nearby, take extra caution when walking alongside a highway.

GETTING TOAD

GETTING TOWED

Chapter 12

Automobile Accidents

What to Do If You Have an Automobile Accident

1. Remain calm. Try not to get hysterical, it only makes things worse. Check for physical injuries to yourself, your passengers, and the people in the other cars involved. Then check for damage to the vehicles.

2. Call the police (tell them you need to file an accident report) and call 911 for an ambulance if people are badly hurt. **Do not leave the scene of the accident!** If there isn't a phone nearby, ask someone who wasn't involved to call the police. In large cities the police won't come out and file a report unless there is an injury.

3. Do not move the cars or try to clean up any broken glass or car bits. The police will need to look at everything to properly fill out the accident report, especially if there is any confusion about who or what caused the accident. If you happen to have a camera, take pictures. Ask

passersby who witnessed the accident to give you their name and phone number.

4. Write down all the details you can remember about what happened. If you are hurt or badly shaken, ask someone to do this for you.

- Names, addresses, and phone numbers of everyone involved (get their work phone number, too!)
- Date, time, and location of the accident.
- Names, addresses, and phone numbers of any witnesses.
- Make, model, color, and license plate numbers of all cars involved.
- Name and phone number of the other party's insurance company.
- Insurance policy number of the other parties involved in the accident.
- Witnesses' names and phone numbers.

5. Do not have a big discussion about who caused the accident. Even if you think the accident was your fault, just give the facts without claiming responsibility. Get the name and badge number of the police officer who filled out the accident report, as well as the file number of your case.

6. Do not say that you are not hurt, because if it turns out later that you have injuries, this may be used against you. If you think you are hurt, see a doctor as soon as possible. The longer you wait,

the harder it may be to prove that your injuries were related to the accident.

7. After filling out an accident report with the police and speaking with your insurance company, call a tow truck for your car, if necessary. If you can't tow your car to a garage and cannot leave it safely parked near the accident scene, you can tow it home until deciding where to bring it for an estimate and repairs. File a report with the insurance company even if it seems as if your car isn't really messed up, because there may be expensive hidden or structural damage that isn't obvious to you.

After an Automobile Accident (Dealing with the Wreckage)

Your claim will not be processed until both auto insurance agents are contacted. Call them both yourself, even if the other party says he will call his agent. Establish a relationship with somebody in both companies so you have personal contacts and can expedite the claims process. If both parties are insured by the same company, it is still a good idea to to talk to the different agents who are representing everyone involved.

If you've only had a minor fender bender, and there is no physical damage to your vehicle, you still must make an appointment to have the car aligned. Any front end or frame damage will show up in the process of aligning the car.

A car that has been in an accident and appears to

have only body damage should nevertheless get checked out by a mechanic, preferably before it goes to the body shop for body work. Some shops do mechanical repairs and body work under the same roof, but you may have to have two different damage reports written up from two different shops. You can get an estimate from a shop of your choosing, but the company that's paying will usually insist on sending out its own estimator. Your insurance agent can refer you to a shop if the accident happened while you were out of town.

Make it very clear that the shop may not proceed with any repairs until you give the go ahead. You may have to wait until you find out how much the insurance company agrees to cover. Most shops charge storage fees, which can be as high as twenty-five dollars per day. Work it out with the insurance company so that they will pay for any storage, especially if they are taking their time in dealing with your case. Be sure to negotiate for a paid rental car while your car is being repaired.

Don't be intimated by insurance companies. They are huge for-profit bureaucracies that want to make as much money as possible. They often try to pay you less than the total damages. This is especially true if your car was totaled in the accident. Be persistent and patient and insist that they pay what the car is worth. This is why you have been paying premiums all these years.

A Few Words about Auto Insurance

The cost of auto insurance seems to keep going up, but if you get in an accident or your car is stolen or damaged, you'll be glad you have it. Here are some ways to bring down the cost of your car insurance.

1. Drive less. If you only use your car for leisure and don't drive very much, tell your insurance agent.
2. Ask about student and senior discounts.
3. Increase your deductible.
4. Buy only liability and uninsured motorist insurance if your car is close to retirement or already banged up.
5. Get a multicar discount by using the same company to insure spouses' and kids' cars.
6. Cars with air bags, passive restraint seat belt systems, and antilock brakes often get a discount.
7. Some cars cost more than others to insure. If you are in the market for a new or used car, check out how much different cars cost to insure.
8. Shop around for the best price!

Auto theft insurance usually does not cover the contents of your trunk, but your homeowner's or rental insurance should. Check with your insurance agent.

Chapter 13

How to Keep Your Car Running Forever

All-Around Preventive Maintenance

Body

- Take care of little dings before there are too many.
- Don't slam the doors.
- Washing your car prevents rust, but don't wash it in direct sunlight.
- Lube all the door hinges every few months.
- Open the sunroof once a week to keep it from sticking.

Brakes

- Always set the parking brake so your car doesn't roll down a hill and hit a BMW.
- Use the ABS (antilock brakes) every couple of

months: intentionally stop short, as when making a panic stop; the brake pedal should pulsate.
- Don't ride the brakes.
- Avoid sudden stops.
- Don't speed up for stop signs.

Clutch

- Have the clutch adjusted regularly (about every six months).
- Don't ride the clutch (when stopped on a hill, don't use the clutch to keep the car from moving backward).
- Put the clutch in Neutral and take your foot off the clutch pedal while waiting at stoplights and stop signs.
- Do not lend your car to bad drivers or someone who is new to driving a manual-transmission car.
- Excessive downshifting will cause the clutch to wear prematurely
- Don't lug the engine; shift at 2,500 rpm.
- Don't shift from forward to reverse while the car is moving.

Engine

- Change the oil and oil filter every 3,000 miles.
- Follow the maintenance schedule in your owner's manual and in this book.
- Don't drive in the redline; 2,500 rpm is best.

- Fix leaks as they happen.
- Use higher octane if the engine pings on hills or acceleration.
- Avoid rapid acceleration.
- Don't rev the engine when starting the car.
- Warm your car up for one minute and drive gently for the first five minutes.
- Don't crank the starter motor longer than twenty seconds.
- Use the air conditioner for ten minutes once a month.

Gas

- Keep the gas tank above a quarter full, especially in winter.
- If the engine pings, use a higher octane gas.

Interior

- Seat covers will protect the seat cushions from getting stained or torn.
- Use vinyl conditioner on the dashboard and other vinyl inside the car to prevent cracking.
- Do not have a big heavy key chain hanging from the ignition switch; the weight will eventually wear the switch, causing the key to get stuck or not work.

Steering and Front End

- On cars with power steering, don't turn the wheel when the engine is off.

- Don't force the wheels against the curb when parking.

Suspension

- Avoid carrying heavy loads around that you don't need to; it's a waste of gas and bad for the car.
- Avoid or slow down for bumps.

Tires

- Replace worn tires before you get a flat.
- Get a front end alignment if the car pulls to one side, before the tires wear out.
- Don't do 360s in empty parking lots late at night.

Transmission

- Service the transmission every two years or 30,000 miles, whichever comes first.
- Do not use fifth gear or overdrive under 45 mph.
- Don't shift from forward to reverse while the car is moving.
- Don't put the car in Neutral at stoplights if you have automatic transmission.
- Towing cars or trailers puts extra strain on a transmission, and may shorten its life.
- Engage and use the four-wheel drive once a month.

Ren's Seven Laws of Auto Repair: (All Scientifically Tested and Proven)

1. If you bring your car into the shop for a noise it will be gone by the time the mechanic drives it.

2. If you stop by the shop to pick up your car without calling first there's a 90 percent chance it won't be ready.

3. If you forget to set the parking brake while parked on a hill, there's a 75 percent chance that if it rolls away it will hit a Mercedes on its way down the hill.

4. If you bring your car to get repaired the day before a big trip, your car will need a part that has to be special ordered from across the country and will take three days to be delivered.

5. If you buy a used car without first getting it checked out by a mechanic, there's a 68 percent chance it'll be a lemon.

6. If you don't know how to change a tire, you'll get a lot of flat tires.

7. If you do know how to change a tire, you'll only get flat tires when you're dressed in your best party dress.

Chapter 14

Selling Your Car

Make It Look Fabulous

1. Clean the interior; or better yet, pay to get the car professionally detailed. Clean the trunk, too.

2. Wash, wax, and shine.

3. Have the engine steam-cleaned.

4. Use the right color touch up paint (available at a body shop) for small nicks in the paint.

5. Fix any drivability problems so it runs smoothly, and repair any leaks.

How Much Is It Worth?

You can do the same research on a car you already own as you would if you were buying a car. Check the *Kelly Blue Book* (at your local bookstore or library) value and look in the paper to see what similar cars are being sold for. Don't ask too much or too little. Most people ask more than they expect to get, and the person who buys it will probably try to bargain and negotiate. Have a bottom-line price in mind, whatever your asking price is.

Where to Sell It

You will always get a better price if you sell to an individual than a dealer. A car dealer will try to buy your car cheap enough so that he can make a profit. This is money you can make if you sell the car yourself. Put an ad in the local paper. Be sure to include all the pertinent information in the ad: year, make, model, mileage, price, your phone number, and when you can be reached.

When people come to look at your car, have a friend with you, because you will be dealing with strangers. You will most likely have to spend some time on the phone and few a Saturdays showing your car and letting people test-drive it. You may want to go on the test-drive with the prospective customer; for safety, bring a friend along, too.

The Paperwork

Have all the records and paperwork available.
1. Title
2. Registration
3. Owner's manual
4. All the previous repair orders
5. Warranty or service contract
6. Emissions or smog certificate (if required in your area)

Bill of Sale

A receipt, or bill of sale, must be drawn up and signed by both the seller (you) and the buyer. It doesn't need to be fancy, but it should include the date, name and address of the person buying the car, year, make and mileage of the car, and the vehicle identification number (VIN). The VIN can be found on the doorjamb of the driver's door or on the dashboard on the driver's side as you look in through the windshield. Be sure to write "AS IS" on the bill of sale, and make two copies, one for you and one for the buyer.

Contact your local department of motor vehicles to notify them of the change of ownership so you won't be liable for any tickets the new owner gets.

Never take a personal check! Ask for cash or a certified check. If you must take a personal check insist that the car not be delivered until the check clears.

Chapter 15

Buying a Used Car

Deciding What You Want

Buying a used car can be daunting. Cars are expensive, sellers often don't reveal the truth, and you want something that is reliable, safe, and makes you look cool. The good news is, as long as you do a little research and don't buy a car on impulse, you'll probably find exactly what you want without too much trouble.

In the last few years Americans purchased more used car than new cars. So don't worry, your perfect car exists and is for sale in your price range. There are thousands of cars out there, new or used. If you narrow your choices down a little it will make it easier when you start looking. Do you want an automatic or manual transmission? A two-door, four-door, hatchback, or wagon? Do you absolutely need power steering or can you live without it? Start thinking about your personal needs and looking at friend's cars. (Also look at the options list and types of cars on page 166.)

Ask your friends about their cars, and ask them if you can test-drive their cars to get a sense of how different cars drive. Go to a used-car lot and ask to test-drive several kinds of cars. They don't all feel the same, so the more cars you drive the better you'll know what you're looking for.

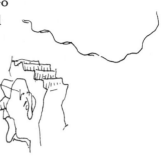

Decide how much money you can spend, including state sales tax, registration, and insurance. Registration and insurance costs vary according to what kind of car you have, too. A sports car will cost more to insure than a family car, for instance. This will also help you narrow down your options. Always arrange financing beforehand with your credit union or bank, especially if you plan to buy from a dealer. New- and used-car dealers make a lot of money on financing, so you'll get a better rate at the bank.

When looking for a car, everyone you ask has opinions about which models are good and which aren't. Ask plenty of questions and take your time. If you do a little homework and don't rush into anything, you'll find the right car. Assuming you want a car that is reliable and needs as little maintenance as possible, you need to avoid the temptation to buy that twenty-year-old Italian sports car that looks very cool. Do you want a dependable car for commuting to work every day or a new weekend job as a mechanic?

Even if a used car seems perfect to you, don't

buy it without checking it out thoroughly. Definitely bring any prospective car to a mechanic to do a prepurchase inspection. Most shops provide this service. But before you bring your prospective car in for a checkover, there are things you can check yourself. Otherwise, you'll end up spending a lot of money and time bringing every car under consideration to your mechanic for a prepurchase inspection.

Buying a used car takes a lot of time. If you need a car before that new job starts or to drive across the country for a long-awaited vacation, give yourself at least two months or longer to find a good used car. Waiting until you're desperate will cloud your judgment and you'll end up with something you don't love. Alternately, don't get your heart set on one particular car. There's always another, better car out there just waiting for you.

Types of Cars

Convertible	Sedan
Coupe	Sports car
Full-size van	Station wagon
Hatchback	Pickup truck
Luxury	Sport Utility vehicle
Minivan	

Options

Decide what you want before going to the dealer so you don't get suckered into stuff you don't need.

Air bags (driver and passenger)

Air conditioning

Antitheft system (car alarm)

Automatic transmission

Antilock brakes

Cruise control

Dashboard gauges: lights, analog gauges, or digital

4×4 (four-wheel drive)

Interior: cloth, leather, etc.

Overdrive (fifth gear)

Power steering

Power locks (to lock and unlock all the doors at once)

Power windows

Rear-window defroster

Roof or luggage rack

Sound system (car stereo)

Sunroof

Tilt steering wheel (adjustable)

Traction control

Turbo

Do a Little Research

The classified section of your local paper will give you an idea of how much you might be spending for the type of car you are looking for. Also look in the *Kelly Blue Book* for prices of used cars, which can be purchased at most bookstores.

Your local library can supply you with a copy of the used-car issue of the magazine *Consumer Reports*, which comes out every April and provides information on used cars.

1. *Kelly Blue Book*: Used Car Guide, consumer edition (published twice each year, in January and July)
2. *Consumer Reports*: April issue
3. *The Used Car Book* by Jack Gillis (Harper and Row, New York 1987)
4. *NADA: National Automobile Dealer's Association Used-Car Guide*
5. *Consumer Reports Used-Car Pricing*: call 900-258-2886; costs about $3.00 a minute
6. AAA Vehicle Pricing Service: (call your local AAA (Automobile Association of America).
7. Helpful Internet Sites:
   - http://www.nada.org/
   - http://www.edmunds.com
   - http://www.autoweb.com/info.htm
   - http://www.traderonline.com
   - http://www.eauto.com

Where to Find Used Cars

Once you've narrowed the choices, it's time to begin looking. You can usually get a better deal from an individual than from a car-lot dealer. Dealers give a lousy price on trade-ins, too. You'll do better to sell your old car yourself, if you have the time. Individuals usually sell through word of mouth, signs posted in local stores, or in the classifieds. The local paper or the local *Auto Trader* paper is a good place to start.

Recently there has been some flurry in the news about used car "superstores." These are large used-car dealerships that offer a big selection and haggle-free prices. Even if you are buying from a dealer, you still need to check each car out very thoroughly, and have a mechanic do a prepurchase inspection. Some dealers offer a limited warranty on certain parts of the car. Make sure you understand exactly what is covered and for how long.

The Internet can also provide you with listings of used cars for sale. Key in "used cars for sale" for several sites on the World Wide Web. You can find listings for individuals and dealers selling used cars. You can also get an idea of the going price for the kind of car you want. The disadvantage of shopping on the Internet is you may find exactly what you are looking for, but it's for sale on the other side of the country.

Leasing companies and rental car companies are another option in the used-car search. Again, always check out any prospective car thoroughly, regardless of how well taken care of it looks. Rental cars and leasing car companies don't always maintain cars as well as they could, and when people rent cars they usually don't take the best care of them.

Some people have had great experiences buying cars from friends, others have reported losing friends as a result of a deal gone bad. If you choose to buy from a friend, be very clear from the start.

It's a good idea to get things in writing, even though you both may feel that you trust each other. Perfectly reasonable people can get strange when it comes to money, and an unclear money transaction can ruin a good friendship. This isn't to say you shouldn't buy a car from a friend. Just make all the terms very clear.

Finally, if you absolutely can't handle the prospect of searching for a used car, you can sign up with an auto search firm. For a set fee you will receive listings of used cars in your price range at area dealers. Getting the car checked out and negotiating the price is still up to you.

Keep in mind that no matter how meticulous you are in your search for the perfect car, you are always taking a chance when buying a used car. Caveat emptor!

What the Abbreviations in Car Ads Stand For

3/4/5/6/8 CYL:	number of cylinders the engine has
2/4 DR:	two or four door
2 WD:	two-wheel drive
4 WD:	four-wheel drive
4 SP(D):	four-speed transmission
5 SP(D):	five-speed transmission (has overdrive)
ABS:	antilock braking system
A/C:	air conditioning
A/T:	automatic transmission

CASS or CD:	stereo system with tape player or CD player
CLN:	clean
CONV:	convertible
DOHC:	double overhead camshaft
EFI:	fuel injection
ENG:	engine
EX or G COND:	in excellent or good condition
FWD:	front-wheel drive
HB:	hatchback
K:	thousands of miles
L:	liter
LB:	long bed (pickup truck)
LTHR:	leather interior
LOADED:	has all the extras and options
MNRF:	moonroof (same as sunroof)
MPG:	miles per gallon
OBO/BO:	best offer (Make them an offer!)
OD:	overdrive
P/U:	pickup truck
PS:	power steering
PW:	power windows
RWD:	rear-wheel drive
S/R or SNRF:	sunroof
STD:	standard transmission (stick shift)
TRANS:	transmission
WGN:	wagon
XTRA CAB:	(in a pickup truck, two small seats in the cab)

Over the Phone

You can save yourself time and money if you ask the right questions over the phone. Keep this list with you as you make phone calls.

1. **"Why are you selling this car?"** If the person hesitates on this question, it might be because it's a lemon, or they just found out it needs major repairs and they want to get rid of it quick.

2. **"How many miles does it have?"** It's best to buy a car with under 100,000 miles on it. The lower the mileage, the better. The more money you have to spend, the lower-mileage car you can buy. Generally, the lower the mileage, the longer you will own it without trouble. Freeway miles are better than city miles, too. A car that has been driven mostly for a commute on the highway will have less wear and tear on the transmission, clutch, brakes, and suspension.

3. **"How many owners has it had?"** If the car has had more than two or three owners, or the seller doesn't know how many people have owned it, you may want to

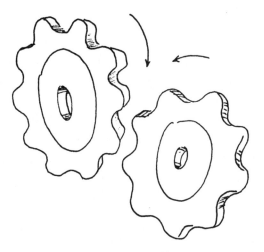

pass this one by. What's wrong with this car that so many people have gotten rid of it?

4. "Do you have the service records?" A car with only one owner and all the service records is a good one to check out. It will be helpful if you buy this car to know what its service history is. If the seller claims it has a new transmission or a rebuilt engine, great, but without any repair orders there's no way to know if it's the truth.

5. "Will you let my mechanic check it out?" Most reasonable people will agree to this unless they have something to hide. Sometimes the owner will allow you to drive the car to your mechanic, or you can agree to meet at the garage *of your choice* while you both wait for it to be checked out. This is an out-of-pocket expense for you, whether you buy the car or not.

6. "Has it ever been in an accident or had any major engine repair?" You want to find out about any major repairs, especially repairs done in the recent past. If the seller claims it has a rebuilt engine or new transmission, make sure he has the receipts. Don't buy a car that's very rusty or has major collision damage, no matter how cheap. Cars that have been in wrecks can have frame damage that may not be visible to you but will be a problem nonetheless.

7. "Have you ever used it for towing anything?" Towing campers or trailers puts extra strain on the transmission, shortening its lifespan.

8. "Do you have all the paperwork?" This will include title and registration, and in some places, smog or emissions certificate and/or inspection certificate. Don't buy a car from someone who isn't the registered owner. If someone is selling a car he doesn't own, it may be because he is a street mechanic who fixes up cars, usually doing as little as possible to make it look good so he can turn a quick profit.

9. "Does it need any work now?" If you can't drive it home, don't buy it. Many older used cars will need some repairs, but ideally you want a car that doesn't have anything wrong with it. If your mechanic tells you it needs some repairs, be sure to find out if the seller will either fix the problem before you buy it or subtract the cost of fixing it from the final price. If a car is really cheap but needs tons of work (a "fixer-upper"), it still may not be a bargain if you add up the time and money you'll spend getting it repaired.

10. "How old are the tires? battery? clutch? When was the last tune-up?" Tires last about three to four years, batteries for five years, and clutches need replacing about every 60,000 miles. Most cars should be tuned-up every 30,000 miles.

Looking at Cars

After you've found a promising car over the phone, make an appointment to look at it. There are plenty of things you can check before bringing the car in for a more thorough inspection by your mechanic. This check is easy and will take you less than thirty minutes, including the test-drive. Look at the car on a clear day; if it's nighttime or raining there might be things you'll miss. Bring a friend along, too—she might be more objective since she's not buying the car.

Also bring a pen and paper (to take notes), your driver's license and copy of your insurance, and a check in case you want to put a deposit on the car.

Leaks: Look under the car and on the pavement for stains or puddles. Look under the hood for major oil leaks. The dryer and cleaner an engine is, the better. Any leaks you find will need to be diagnosed and repaired if you buy this car.

Body: Look for fenders or hoods with paint that doesn't match the rest of the car, or a new paint job on a late-model car. These can be signs of a car that's been in an accident. Look for major rust, especially underneath the car. Look for rust or leaks inside the car, especially the trunk. Dampness or a musty smell in the car or trunk is a sign that when it rains water is leaking into the car. Bring a small magnet with you: A magnet will not stick to "bondo," which is used in body repairs. This is a good way to find out if major repairs have been made to fenders, body panels, doors, and hoods. If the car has a "bra" on the front end (leather or vinyl covering), take it off and inspect underneath for signs of body damage or previous body work.

Tires: Make sure all the tires are in good condition. Look for uneven tire wear and shallow tread. Good, new tires cost at least fifty dollars and up each. Check that the spare tire is in decent condition, and that all the parts for changing a tire come with the car: jack, lugnut wrench, spare tire). See Chapter 5 for more on how to evaluate tire condition.

Interior: Try out all the interior hardware and accessories: door handles, seat belts, dome lights, clock, cigarette lighter, window controls, radio, heater and air conditioning, windshield wipers and washer, etc. Make sure the seats adjust. Have your friend look while you try out all the lights, directionals, high beams, backup and brake lights. Check the seats for tears and sagging cushions. Check out every gadget the car has, even ones you think you'll never need or use.

Test-drive: Before you start the car put the key to the On position. All the dashboard lights should light up (engine light, charge light, brake light, oil light etc.). It is important that these lights operate, because their function is to alert the driver of any problems while driving. Gauges work only when the car is running, so check those, too.

The car should start up easily and idle smoothly. Be sure to take it for a drive on the highway. Test-drive it hard—go fast, stop short, drive on a winding road. Try a few steep hills. Does it have good power? Listen for squeaks and rattles. Make sure it doesn't pull to one side when you brake. Write down everything you notice on your test-drive.

Rest your hands lightly on the steering wheel for a few seconds as you're going down the road and make sure the car doesn't pull to one direction. The brakes should be able to stop the car short without too much effort, they shouldn't be soft or spongy, and they shouldn't sink to the floor when you press down. These are some indications that the car needs some immediate attention.

If your prospective car passes all the earlier checks (telephone interview, test-drive, and your own visual inspection), the next step is to have a mechanic check it out. Write down anything you notice so you can ask your mechanic to pay special attention to those things.

Pre-Purchase Inspection

Many shops offer a service that allows you to bring in a car you don't yet own for a prepurchase inspection. Do not buy a used car without having a mechanic check it out first!

A one-hour inspection is usually sufficient. Here is a list of the things your mechanic should check.

- Test-drive: check general operation of transmission, clutch, brakes, steering, acceleration, suspension.
- Cylinder compression check: Make sure a *compression test* is done, not a cylinder *balance test*. The cylinder balance test is not as accurate.
- Check for oil leaks.
- Load-test battery and check charging system.
- Visual inspection of cooling system and pressure test cooling system.
- Check tire condition.
- Check front end and suspension.
- Check exhaust system.

- Put the car on the oscilloscope to check ignition system.
- Check the emissions using a three-gas analyzer (smog machine) to check the fuel and emissions system.

Negotiating the Final Price

If you decide to buy the car, have your mechanic give you an estimate of any repairs it needs. You can either ask the seller to make these repairs first, or subtract the cost from the final price. Don't sign anything or hand over any money until you get this in writing.

Most people selling cars ask for more than what they expect to get. Don't be afraid to bargain. Some car lot dealers will not lower the asking price, regardless of what you find wrong with the car. They can't sell a car any cheaper than what they originally paid. An individual, on the other hand, may be willing to significantly reduce the price. For some people, offering cash is another incentive for lowering the price.

After a price has been agreed upon, don't forget to ask for all the necessary paperwork:

- Title
- Bill of sale *
- Owner's manual
- All repair orders
- Smog or emissions certificate (in some areas)
- Warranty in writing (if from a dealer)

---

*Resist the temptation to hide some tax money from Uncle Sam by having the seller write a lower selling price on the bill of sale. If you ever get in an accident and the car is totaled, you will have a difficult time recouping the real value of the car from the insurance company.

Glossary

ABS: See anti-lock brake system.

accessories: Devices that your car does not need to run, but make your ride nicer, for example, the radio or power windows.

air bags: Safety devices used on either or both the driver's side and the passenger's side to protect riders from injury. The bags inflate if the car is impacted.

air filter: Filters dust and dirt from the air that the engine uses.

amps (amperes): A measurement of electrical flow.

alignment (or wheel alignment): An adjustment made to the front end (and in some cars, the rear end) components to ensure that the wheels are correctly lined up with the road and with each other.

alternator: A device in your car that recharges the battery when the engine is running. The alternator is driven by a belt (which is driven by the engine) and supplies electricity to the battery and other accessories.

antifreeze: A liquid used in the radiator and cooling system to keep the engine from getting too hot or freezing.

anti-lock brakes: A braking system that is electronically monitored by a computer to prevent the brakes from locking up if the driver slams on the brakes.

ASE: Automotive Society of Engineers.

ATF (automatic transmission fluid): A lubricating fluid used in automatic transmissions and in some power steering systems.

automatic transmission: A transmission that changes the gears for you, as opposed to having a clutch pedal and stick shift.

axle: A shaft that connects the power from the transmission to the wheels.

battery: An electrochemical device that stores electricity.

battery load test: A test done by mechanics to check battery charge.

belts: Rubber belts that use the engine's power to turn other devices like the alternator, the power-steering pump, the air conditioner, the water pump, the fan, and the smog pump.

brake pad: The part of the brakes that is pressed against the brake rotor to stop the car. On cars with disk brakes, each wheel has two brake pads.

brake rotor: Part of the brake system on cars with disk brakes; a metal disk that spins with the wheel.

brake shoes: Part of the brake system on cars with drum brakes that presses against the brake drums to stop the car.

caliper: The part of the disk brakes that squeezes the brake pads together when you step on the brake pedal, causing the car to stop.

carburetor: A device that mixes the air and fuel before it reaches the engine. All cars are either carbureted or fuel injected.

catalytic converter: A part of the exhaust system, located between the engine and the muffler, that cleans harmful exhaust gasses by creating a chemical reaction between a catalyst and the exhaust gas.

chassis: The metal frame of a car (pronounced like "classy").

choke: In cars with carburetors, the choke cuts off (or "chokes") the air when the engine is cold so that there is a richer air-fuel mixture (more gas, less air), and the car runs smoother.

clutch: The system in a manual-transmission car that transmits the power from the engine to the transmission.

combustion: The process of gasoline burning inside the engine's cylinders.

coolant: A mixture of antifreeze and water in the radiator and cooling system that prevents over-heating.

coolant reservoir: A container for extra or overflow coolant that is connected to the radiator via a tube or hose.

CV boot: A flexible rubber boot that protects the CV joint by keeping grease in and dirt out.

CV joint: A joint that allows the wheels to turn at the same rate of speed when the car is going around corners; there are two constant velocity joints on each axle of a front-wheel-drive car.

cylinder block: The lower part of the engine where the cylinders, pistons, and crankshaft are located. The engine may have any number of cylinders (3, 4, 5, 6, or 8, for example) depending on the design.

cylinder head: The top part of the engine where the valves are located.

dealership: Where new cars are sold and repaired.

diesel: A type of fuel (actually a light oil) that is used in diesel engines.

differential: On rear-wheel-drive cars, a set of gears that allow both wheels to spin at the same speed when the car is turning corners.

dipstick: A long, thin metal stick used for measuring fluid levels.

disk brakes: A brake system that has a brake disk (or brake rotor) at each wheel, that spins with the wheel. Brake pads are squeezed against the rotor by a hydraulic caliper to stop the car.

distributor cap: A plastic part in the ignition system that covers the distributor, with spark plus wires connected to the top of it.

distributorless ignition: An ignition system in newer cars that does not have a distributor; instead the computer does the job of distributing the spark.

distributor rotor: A plastic part inside the distributor that spins to distribute the spark.

DOM: The date of manufacture, which can be found on the driver's side door jam.

DOT: Department of Transportation.

drain plug: A bolt that can be removed to drain fluid.

drive shaft: A metal shaft that connects the power from the transmission to the wheels.

drum brakes: A type of brake system that uses brake shoes and brake drums. Many older cars (pre-1970) have four wheel drum brakes. Some newer cars have four wheel disk brakes. It is common for cars to have disk brakes in the front and drum brakes in the rear.

ECM: Electronic Control Module—the computer, or brain, of modern cars.

ECU: Electronic Control Unit—as above, the computer, or brain, of modern cars.

electric fan: A fan that cools the radiator, and gets its power from the battery.

electrolyte: A corrosive liquid in the battery made of sulfuric acid and water.

emission control system: The various devices in your car that control and reduce the amount of harmful gases the engine produces.

engine block: The bottom half of the engine where the cylinders, pistons, and crankshaft are located.

exhaust system: The pipes and devices that funnel the burnt gases away from the engine and into the air.

fan: A device that cools the radiator. The cooling fan is either driven by a belt or is powered by the battery.

firing order: The order in which the spark plugs fire, or spark, in each cylinder.

four by four: Another word for four-wheel drive, which is a car or truck that has power going to all four wheels.

four-wheel drive: When the power from the engine is sent to all four wheels.

front-wheel drive: When the power from the engine goes only to the front wheels.

fuel filter: A device that filters out dirt and dust from the gasoline before it reaches the engine.

fuel injection: A fuel delivery system in which fuel injectors squirt gasoline directly into each cylinder. All cars are either carbureted or fuel injected.

fuel pump: The device that pumps fuel from the gas tank to the engine.

fuse: A thin metal strip that protects the car's electrical equipment by breaking, or "blowing," if too much current passes through it.

gasket: A thin piece of material which seals two metal parts that are bolted together.

gasoline: The combustible liquid that burns inside the engine to create the heat (power) that drives your car.

gear oil: A thick oil that lubricates the gears in the transmission and the differential.

ground: Part of the electrical circuit. The connection of any electrical device to the engine or body of the car allows the electricity to return to its source, thereby completing the circuit.

head: See cylinder head.

head gasket: The gasket that sits between the top half and the bottom half of the engine and prevents compressed air in the cylinders from escaping and keeps coolant from mixing with the gasoline.

idle: When the engine is running, but your foot is not on the gas and the transmission is in neutral.

jack: A tool used to raise up a car.

jack stands: Metal stands that mechanics use to hold up a car after it has been jacked up, so it is safe to climb under.

jump-start: Using the battery from another car

and a set of jumper cables to get a car started when it has a dead battery.

loaded: A car that has all kinds of fancy options like leather seats and stereo speakers, etc.

load test: A test a mechanic does to determine how much charge your battery has.

lube: When a mechanic uses grease to keep certain components moving freely.

lugnut: The nuts that hold the tires on.

manual transmission: See standard transmission.

manufacturer: The company that originally designed and built a certain brand car.

master cylinder: The main part of the hydraulic-braking system that includes the brake-fluid reservoir.

mph: Miles per hour or rate of speed.

mpg: Miles per gallon; how many miles your car can go on one gallon of gasoline.

muffler: A device that quiets, or "muffles," the sound in the exhaust system so your car doesn't sound really loud.

octane rating: A measurement of the anti-knock qualities of gasoline.

OEM: Original equipment manufactured, or parts that were made by the same company that built the car.

odometer: A meter on the dashboard that measures the RPMs, or revolutions per minutes, of your engine.

OHC: Overhead camshaft.

oil: A petroleum product that is used to lubricate moving metal parts in your engine and transmission.

oil filter: The component that filters dust and particles from the oil.

oil pump: The device that pumps the oil from the oil pan to the rest of the engine.

owner's manual: The small book that comes with every new car explaining the details of the car and outlining the maintenance the car will need.

oxygen sensor: A device in the exhaust manifold that measures the oxygen in the exhaust gases and sends this information to the car's computer, so the computer can make a decision about whether to send a richer or leaner air/gas mixture to the engine.

parking brake: The brake that you set by hand or foot, also called the emergency brake.

PCV valve: The positive crankcase ventilation valve is a small plastic valve that allows fumes in the top half of the engine to be sucked back into the engine to be burned, decreasing the amount of pollutants released by the car.

pinging: A sound from the engine similar to shaking a can of popcorn in a glass jar. Pinging indicates that your car needs either a higher octane gasoline or the ignition timing is too advanced.

psi: Pounds per square inch.

radiator: The device that helps to remove heat from the cooling system as coolant passes through it.

radiator cap: The cap that keeps the coolant under pressure inside your radiator.

rear-wheel drive: When the power from the engine is transmitted to the rear wheels only.

rebuilt: See remanufactured.

recall: When the manufacturer takes the responsibility for a failed part and agrees to fix all affected cars at their expense.

remanufactured: A part that has been rebuilt so it can be sold and used as a replacement part.

repair order: The paperwork that documents the work done on a car while it is at a repair shop. The repair order serves as a written estimate and a receipt.

rpm: Revolutions per minute.

SAE: Society of Automotive Engineers.

sensor: Any device in your car that gathers information from a part of the car or engine and sends this information back to the car's computer.

service writer: The person who sits behind the desk and answers phones and talks to customers at an auto repair shop.

shock absorbers: Part of the suspension system that makes for easier handling and a smoother ride.

short: When electricity takes a short cut to ground, instead of going the way it was supposed to, resulting in something not working.

smog check: When exhaust gases and emissions components are checked to make sure the car is not polluting excessively.

spark plug: A part that provides the spark inside the engine's cylinders which ignites the fuel.

spark-plug wires: A cable that delivers the spark

from the distributor cap to the spark plugs.

stall: When the engine shuts off unexpectedly.

standard transmission: A transmission for which the driver must manually shift the gears by using a clutch pedal and a gear stick.

starter motor: An electrical motor that cranks the engine to get it started.

strut: A type of shock absorber where the shock and the spring are combined together.

synthetic oil: Chemically created oil, not derived from natural petroleum.

tachometer: A gauge on the dashboard that measures rpm (revolutions per minute) or engine speed.

tailpipe: The last part of the exhaust system after the muffler, at the back of the car, which routes exhaust gases away from the car.

thermostat: A device that regulates temperature and the flow of liquid, air, or gas.

throttle: A device controlled by the driver (via the gas pedal) that determines the engine's speed.

timing (ignition timing): When the ignition spark enters the cylinder.

timing belt: The internal rubber belt that connects the top half of the engine (the camshaft) with the bottom half (the crankshaft).

timing chain: The internal metal chain that connects the top half of the engine (the camshaft) with the bottom half (the crankshaft).

torque: A measurement of twisting force.

traction: How well tires grip the road.

transaxle: The transmission in a front-wheel-drive car.

transfer case: The gears in a four-wheel-drive car that connect the front-wheel drive with the rear-wheel drive.

transmission: A set of gears that transmit power from the engine to the wheels.

transmission fluid: The lubricating fluid inside the transmission, also referred to as ATF, or automatic transmission fluid.

tread: The grooves in tires.

tread depth gauge: A tool that is used to measure the thickness of the treads in a car tire.

Index

Important Car Information

Emergency Numbers:

Your mechanic
_____

Emergency roadside service
_____

Wealthy aunt
_____

Your therapist
_____

Your Car's Stats:

Year
_____

Make
_____

Model
_____

Engine Size
_____

License #
_____

VIN (Vehicle Identification #)
_____

Insurance:

Company Name
_____

Company Telephone #
_____

Policy #
_____